ideas

ideas

storage
para guardar
rangement
aufbewahren

AUTHORS
Fernando de Haro & Omar Fuentes

EDITORIAL DESIGN & PRODUCTION

ARQUITECTOS
EDITORES
MEXICANOS

PROJECT MANAGERS
Valeria Degregorio Vega
Tzacil Cervantes Ortega

COORDINATION
Susana Madrigal Gutiérrez
Adriana García Hernández

COPYWRITER
Roxana Villalobos

ENGLISH TRANSLATION
Louis Loizides

FRENCH TRANSLATION
Cécile Usselmann (Centro Profesional de Traducción e Interpretación / IFAL)

GERMAN TRANSLATION
Heike Ruttkowski

Ideas
storage · para guardar · rangement · aufbewahren

© 2007, Fernando de Haro & Omar Fuentes

AM Editores S.A. de C.V.
Paseo de Tamarindos 400 B, suite 102, Col. Bosques de las Lomas,
C.P. 05120, México, D.F. Tels. 52(55) 5258 0279, Fax. 52(55) 5258 0556.
E-mail: ame@ameditores.com   www.ameditores.com

ISBN 10: 970-9726-65-X
ISBN 13: 978-970-9726-65-7

Printed in China.

INDEX • INDICE

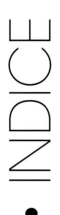

introduction • introducción • introduction • einleitung 8

introduction   introducción

STORING something means taking care of it, watching over it or protecting it; it can also mean putting it in a safe place. However, for architects and interior designers storing something is more than just this; it reflects a need to maintain a certain order in space.

Nowadays, the aim of design, in addition to maintaining order, is to propose a new way of looking at how we store things and encourage users to make the most of space through an approach centered on educational games; this is why furniture and places for keeping

Guardar significa tener cuidado de algo, vigilarlo y defenderlo; o bien colocar algún objeto en donde esté seguro. Sin embargo, para arquitectos e interioristas el guardado supera esta definición y también se relaciona con la necesidad de mantener orden en el espacio.

El diseño de ahora pretende, además del orden, contribuir a un enfoque novedoso en el acto de guardar e invitar al usuario a sacarle provecho al espacio mediante una actitud

introduction

einleitung

RANGER signifie pour nous mettre un objet à l'abri, le mettre à sa place ; pour les architectes et les décorateurs, rangement et organisation de l'espace sont deux idées qui vont de pair.

L'ordre reste l'un des soucis des designers actuels qui sont toujours en quête de nouvelles idées en matière de rangement. Leur but est de nous inviter à mieux tirer parti de l'espace et de le faire dans un esprit ludique ; en ce sens, la conception de mobilier et d'espaces de rangement représente un challenge. Il n'est pas

AUFBEWAHREN bedeutet auf etwas aufpassen, etwas bewachen oder es verteidigen, bzw. ein Objekt anbringen, in dem es sicher ist. Dennoch geht diese Definition für Architekten und Innenarchitekten viel weiter und wird ausserdem mit der Notwendigkeit in Zusammenhang gebracht, Ordnung zu halten.

Das heutige Design zielt darauf ab, neben der Ordnung auch einen neuen Blickwinkel in Bezug auf das Aufbewahren zu schaffen und den Benutzer dazu zu bewegen, den Platz auf spielerische Art und Weise

things tend to pose a challenge to designers. Bolstering the visual appeal, sophistication, functionality and variety, as well as affording spaciousness and practicality, is no easy task.

The key, without doubt, lies in maximum exploitation of usable space. Modular furniture that can be stowed away or put on wheels increases spatial flexibility; items embedded in the walls are very useful and free up zones of movement; at the same time, furniture designed with a dual function, such as beds with drawers for keeping things, or trunks and furniture that, in addition to storing items, also offer seating, help optimize use of available space.

Some furniture and storage areas are created for specific purposes, such as keeping clothes, documents, objects, shopping or tools; but others, without being set aside

lúdica; por ello, actualmente el mueble y las áreas de guardado en general representan un desafío para los diseñadores. Intentar reforzar su estética, sofisticación, funcionalidad y variedad, aportando espacialidad y practicidad a su uso, no es tarea sencilla.

Sin duda, la clave se encuentra en la máxima explotación del espacio útil. Los muebles modulares que se pueden estibar o aquéllos sobre ruedas incrementan la flexibilidad espacial; los empotrados en la periferia de los muros son de gran utilidad y dejan libres las zonas de circulación; en tanto que los que son planeados con doble función, como es el caso de camas con cajoneras para guardar cosas o baúles y muebles que además de servir para almacenar funcionan como asientos, facilitan el aprovechamiento del área.

simple en effet de conjuguer fonctionnalité, spatialité et aspects pratiques avec sophistication, valeur esthétique et variété.

La solution est probablement d'exploiter au mieux l'espace disponible. On peut obtenir plus de flexibilité grâce aux meubles modulaires et aux meubles montés sur roulettes. Les meubles arrimés aux murs, outre qu'ils sont très utiles, ont l'avantage de ne pas encombrer les zones de circulation, tandis que les meubles comme les lits à tiroirs, les coffres et les banquettes permettent, grâce à leur double fonction de meuble et d'espace de rangement, d'utiliser au mieux l'espace disponible dans une pièce.

Bien que généralement les meubles et autres espaces de rangement soient créés pour des fonctions spécifiques telles que ranger des vêtements, classer

zu nutzen. Daher bedeuten heute die Möbel und die Bereiche zum Aufbewahren im Allgemeinen eine Herausforderung für die Designer. Der Versuch, die Ästhetik, Spitzfindigkeit, Funktionalität und Vielfalt zu verbessern und gleichzeitig auf praktische Weise Raum zu schaffen, ist keine leichte Aufgabe.

Ohne Zweifel geht es darum, den nutzbaren Raum so gross wie eben möglich zu gestalten. Modulmöbel, die verstellt werden können und Möbel auf Rädern erhöhen die räumliche Flexibilität. Einbauschränke, die an der Wand hängen, sind von grossem Nutzen, da so die Arbeitsbereiche frei bleiben. Auch Möbel, die mit doppelter Funktion geplant wurden -wie Betten mit Schubladen zum Aufbewahren von Gegenständen oder Truhen und Möbel, die ausser zum Aufbewahren auch als Sitz dienen- verbessern die Nutzbarkeit der Bereiche.

for storing specific things, offer generous and versatile spaces, of different shapes and sizes, and can store a whole range of things.

In any case, the space or item of furniture assigned the task of storing things must have a unitary and functional look, and be comprised of several containers with compartments in accordance with the type of objects stored.

However, what really stands out in an item of furniture or storage area is shape and volume, which means the need to preserve the sensation of space must be borne in mind when choosing them. In fact, storage areas should slip by unnoticed and let the objects around them take the credit. It is also necessary to gauge how each component of the storage system is supported and make sure it is up to the task at hand.

Aunque por lo común los muebles y demás espacios de guardado son creados para funciones específicas: almacenar ropa, archivar documentos, depositar artículos, despensa o herramientas..., existen también los que sin tener predeterminado un "qué guardar" ofrecen generosos y versátiles espacios, de distintas formas y proporciones, que cumplen con la función de poder almacenar en ellos una gran variedad de cosas.

En cualquiera de los casos, el mueble o el espacio de guardado debe verse como un sistema unitario y funcional, y constituirse de una variedad de contenedores con compartimentos que sean correspondientes con la escala de los objetos que resguardarán.

Por otro lado, lo que resulta más evidente en un mueble o en una zona de almacenaje son su forma y volumen, por lo que al decidirse por ellos se debe cuidar que no estorben la percepción del espacio. De hecho, las áreas de guardado deben pasar desapercibidas y dejar que los objetos a su alrededor se lleven el crédito. Asimismo, conviene evaluar la técnica de soporte de cada pieza que compone al sistema y procurar que su materialidad privilegie su vida útil.

des documents, stocker des denrées alimentaires ou des outils, il en existe d'autres plus versatiles, de formes et de proportions diverses, qui n'ont pas de fonction précise mais qui ne constituent pas moins de généreux espaces de rangement, prêts à accueillir toute sorte d'objets.

Dans tous les cas, le meuble de rangement ou l'ensemble modulaire doit être est vu comme un système unitaire et fonctionnel et être constitué de compartiments variés adaptés aux objets qu'il abritera.

D'autre part, un meuble se distingue de par sa forme et ses volumes ; pour le choisir, on doit donc penser à la pièce qui l'accueillera et veiller à ce qu'il ne soit pas trop encombrant et à ce qu'il ne gâche pas la perception de l'espace. Il est toujours préférable que les espaces de rangement passent inaperçus afin que le regard se porte sur les autres objets présents dans la pièce. Il faut en outre réfléchir à la technique qu'on choisira pour disposer ou fixer les meubles et choisir des matériaux susceptibles de prolonger leur vie utile.

Im Allgemeinen sind Möbel und sonstige Stauräume für spezielle Funktionen geschaffen, wie die Lagerung von Kleidung, Archivierung von Dokumenten, Aufbewahrung von Gegenständen, Lebensmitteln oder Werkzeugen usw. Aber ausserdem gibt es noch diejenigen Möbel, die ohne einen vorbestimmten Aufbewahrungszweck weiträumigen und flexiblen Stauraum mit verschiedenen Formen und Proportionen bieten und dazu dienen, in ihnen eine grosse Vielfalt an Dingen aufzubewahren.

In jedem Fall muss das Möbel oder der Stauraum aussehen wie ein einheitliches und funktionelles System und über eine Vielfalt an Einheiten mit Fächern verfügen, die dem Umfang der Objekte entsprechen, die darin aufbewahrt werden sollen.

Andererseits sind natürlich auch die Form und die Grösse von Möbeln oder Stauräumen ausschlaggebend. Daher ist bei der Auswahl darauf zu achten, dass sie nicht den Gesamteindruck des Raumes stören. Die Stauräume sollten unauffällig sein und nicht den Blick auf sich ziehen. Ausserdem ist es angebracht, die Qualität eines jeden Systemelementes zu prüfen und darauf zu achten, dass das Material eine lange Nutzungsdauer möglich macht.

kitchens and dining rooms
cocinas y comedores
cuisines et salles à manger
küchen und esszimmer

cupboards
alacenas
placards
vorratsschränke

A KITCHEN with sufficient storage space is ideal for keeping clean and tidy. Cupboards, drawers, cabinets and shelves are items of furniture as well as options for storing or keeping things in the kitchen. When you choose them it is advisable to consider their functionality, practicality, spaciousness, depth, proportions, opening and closing system, the number of compartments and the variability of heights, as well as the resilience and ease of cleaning of the materials they are made of, their physical appearance and design.

UNA COCINA que cuente con suficiente espacio de guardado se presta para que se mantenga ordenada y limpia. Alacenas, cajoneras, gabinetes, anaqueles, repisas y estantes son muebles y elementos destinados al almacenaje y guardado en la cocina. Entre las consideraciones que deben tomarse en cuenta al elegirlos están su funcionalidad, practicidad, amplitud, profundidad, proporción, sistema de apertura y cerrado, número de compartimentos y variabilidad de alturas, así como la duración y facilidad de limpieza de los materiales con los que están fabricados, su estética y diseño.

UNE CUISINE dotée d'espaces de rangement en nombre suffisant restera plus facilement propre et bien rangée. Placards, caissons, tiroirs, étagères et présentoirs sont les meubles de rangement dont vous aurez besoin. Pour les choisir, pensez entre autres choses à leur fonctionnalité, à leur aspect pratique, à leurs dimensions, à leur profondeur et à leurs proportions ; examinez également les systèmes de fermeture, le nombre de compartiments, les possibilités de réglage des étagères, les matériaux de fabrication, leur solidité et leur facilité d'entretien ; ne négligez pas, bien entendu, le design et l'aspect esthétique.

EINE KÜCHE, die über ausreichenden Stauraum verfügt, kann leichter ordentlich und sauber gehalten werden. Vorratsschränke, Schubladen, Schränke, Regale, Konsolen und Borde sind Möbel und Elemente, die zur Lagerung und zum Aufbewahren in der Küche dienen. Unter den Aspekten, die bei deren Auswahl in Betracht gezogen werden sollten, befinden sich ihre Funktionalität, Zweckmässigkeit, Ausmass, Tiefe, Proportion, Schliesssystem, Anzahl der Fächer, Verstellbarkeit von Höhen sowie die Dauer und Eignung in Bezug auf die Reinigung der Materialien, mit denen sie gefertigt wurden. Weitere Aspekte stellen die Ästhetik und das Design dar.

Kitchen furniture should be designed in accordance with the space available and particular needs. Storage spaces must be planned to make sure the amount, size and rotation of utensils and foods each of us uses are ideal; any with a high degree of rotation due to frequent usage must be kept in accessible items of furniture that allow them to be seen easily; goods with a low degree of rotation can be kept in high cabinets. In any case, the furniture should not be more than 60 centimeters deep.

Conviene que el mobiliario de cocina se diseñe a la medida del espacio y atendiendo a las necesidades particulares. Planear los lugares de guardado en relación con la cantidad, tamaño y rotación de los utensilios y alimentos con los que cada uno trabaje es ideal; aquéllos que tengan una rotación alta por la frecuencia con que son usados deben guardarse en muebles accesibles y que permitan su rápida visualización; los de baja rotación pueden ubicarse en gabinetes altos. En cualquier caso, la profundidad de los muebles no deberá superar los 60 centímetros.

Il vaut mieux que vos meubles de cuisine soient fabriqués sur mesure en tenant compte de vos besoins spécifiques. L'idéal est de planifier les espaces de rangement en fonction du nombre et de la taille de vos ustensiles de cuisine ainsi que des produits et des aliments que vous consommez. Tenez également compte de la fréquence avec laquelle vous utilisez les objets : placez ceux que vous utilisez le plus couramment à portée de main et de façon à pouvoir les retrouver facilement et réservez le haut des placards aux objets que vous utilisez rarement. En règle générale, vos meubles ne devront pas avoir une profondeur supérieure à 60 cm.

Es ist angebracht, dass die Küchenmöbel nach Mass gefertigt werden, wobei die jeweiligen Anforderungen zu berücksichtigen sind. Am besten ist es, wenn die Stauräume in Übereinstimmung mit der Menge, Grösse und dem Umschlag der Geräte und Nahrungsmittel geplant werden, mit denen jeder Einzelne arbeitet; diejenigen, die einen hohen Umschlag aufweisen und häufig gebraucht werden, sollten in zugänglichen Möbeln aufbewahrt werden, damit sie schnell gesehen werden; und diejenigen mit wenig Umschlag können in Hochschränken aufbewahrt werden. In jedem Falle sollte die Tiefe der Schränke 60 Zentimeter nicht überschreiten.

Wall cupboards and extractible baskets are a good option for make optimum use of space, as is hanging racks or narrow shelves from the doors for keeping smaller products.

Les placards encastrés et les tiroirs coulissants permettent d'exploiter au mieux l'espace disponible ; vous pouvez aussi accrocher des supports ou des tablettes à l'intérieur des portes des placards pour y ranger des objets de petite taille.

Les aliments doivent être conservés à l'abri de l'humidité et de préférence au centre de la cuisine. Veillez à ce que l'ouverture des portes des placards ne gêne pas la circulation.

Einbauvorratsschränke und herausnehmbare Körbe stellen eine Lösung zur optimalen Nutzung des Platzes dar. Ferner können in den Türen Gitter oder schmale Regale angebracht werden, um dort kleine Produkte aufzubewahren.

Shelves for shopping must be spaced out with different depths, sizes and capacities, but they must be placed in a way that respects the height between the knees and the eyes.

Los estantes de las despensas deben estar escalonados con distintas profundidades, tamaños y capacidades, pero en su colocación se tendrá que respetar la altura entre la rodilla y los ojos.

Vos placards doivent être équipés d'étagères de profondeur, de capacité et de dimensions différentes. Pensez toutefois à les placer à une hauteur comprise entre vos yeux et vos genoux.

Die Regale der Vorratsschränke sollten stufenartig angeordnet sein und verschiedene Tiefen, Grössen und Fassungsvermögen aufweisen. Ferner sollten sie auf einer Höhe zwischen Knie und Auge angebracht werden.

KITCHEN COVERINGS may be a continuation of the sink or the cooker, or they could be installed on a work surface. You can put cabinets and drawers underneath them for keeping utensils and ingredients that are used often to prepare food. Coverings, cabinets and drawers should all be spacious, made with tough, non-porous materials, seamless, as well as waterproof and resistant against stains and high temperatures. The surface should also be smooth and easy to clean.

LAS CUBIERTAS DE COCINA pueden ser una continuación de la tarja o de la estufa, o bien estar instaladas en una isla de trabajo. Debajo de ellas es posible colocar gabinetes y cajones para el guardado de los utensilios e ingredientes cuyo uso es frecuente en la preparación de alimentos.

Conviene que tanto cubiertas como gabinetes y cajones sean amplios, de material durable, no poroso, sin juntas, resistente al agua, manchas y temperatura elevada; y que su superficie sea lisa y de fácil aseo.

LE PLAN DE TRAVAIL d'une cuisine peut être installé soit dans la prolongation de la cuisinière ou de l'évier soit sur un meuble à part, placé au centre de la cuisine. Il est utile de placer sous le plan de travail des petits placards et des tiroirs où ranger les ustensiles ou les ingrédients fréquemment utilisés. Il est préférable que le plan de travail, les buffets et les tiroirs soient de bonne taille ; choisir des matériaux durables et non poreux, résistants à l'eau et aux températures élevées. La surface doit être lisse, facile à nettoyer et sans jointures.

DIE ARBEITSFLÄCHEN DER KÜCHE können eine Weiterführung der Spüle oder des Herdes sein oder sich auf einer Arbeitsinsel befinden. Darunter können Schränke und Schubladen zum Aufbewahren von Geräten und Zutaten angebracht werden, die häufig zur Zubereitung der Nahrungsmittel Verwendung finden. Es ist angebracht, dass sowohl die Arbeitsflächen als auch die Schränke und Schubladen gross und aus einem beständigen Material gefertig sind, das nicht porös ist und auch keine Nähte aufweist. Dabei ist auch auf eine Beständigkeit gegen Wasser, Flecken und hohe Temperaturen zu achten; ferner sollte die Oberfläche glatt und leicht zu reinigen sein.

preparation areas
áreas de preparación
plans de travail
arbeitsbereiche

It is the finishes that set the tone of a kitchen, but the style lies in the furniture. This is why it is important to make sure the different items of furniture are related and blend visually. Given that this space is dominated by the storage furniture, care should be taken with its esthetic value. In this regard, the overall set of materials comprising it is just as important as the decorations or the absence of decorations, the handles and the fastening systems that enable them to work.

Aunque son los acabados los que definen la atmósfera de una cocina, los muebles establecen su estilo. Por esta razón, es importante que las diversas piezas del mobiliario se relacionen y coincidan en un patrón visual. Dado que son los muebles de guardado los que dominan este espacio, se debe de cuidar su valor estético. En este sentido, pesan tanto en el conjunto general los materiales de los que están hechos, como sus adornos o la carencia de ellos, las jaladeras y los sistemas de sujeción que permiten que funcionen.

Bien que l'aspect des surfaces joue un rôle déterminant dans la définition de l'ambiance qui règnera dans votre cuisine, les meubles lui apporteront un style particulier. Il est donc important de les choisir de façon à ce qu'ils constituent un ensemble cohérent et agréable à l'œil. Étant donné que par définition ce sont les meubles de rangement qui dominent une cuisine, leurs qualités esthétiques ne doivent pas être négligées. Ainsi, les matériaux dont ces meubles sont faits auront la même importance sur l'aspect d'ensemble que leurs accessoires, poignées et pendants.

Obwohl die Oberflächen die Atmosphäre in einer Küche ausmachen, sind die Möbel jedoch für den Stil verantwortlich. Aus diesem Grunde ist es wichtig, dass die verschiedenen Möbelstücke zusammenpassen und eine visuelle Gesamtheit bilden. Da die Möbel zum Aufbewahren in diesem Bereich vorherrschend sind, ist auf ihren ästhetischen Wert zu achten. In diesem Sinne sind sowohl sämtliche Materialen ausschlaggebend, aus denen die Möbel gefertigt sind, als auch deren vorhandenen oder nicht vorhandenen Verzierungen sowie die Griffe und Befestigungssysteme, die deren Funktion ermöglichen.

A well-designed kitchen makes rational use of all the options of the space. Modular systems are solutions that make it possible to design storage spaces with different configurations. If the shelves are deep, they can be designed in a way that allows them to be pulled out on opening the doors, or moved on rails; this makes the back of the shelves easier to reach.

Una cocina bien diseñada aprovecha racionalmente todas las alternativas del espacio. Los sistemas modulares son soluciones que permiten diseñar espacios de guardado con diferentes configuraciones. Si las repisas son profundas deben diseñarse de forma que puedan extraerse al abrir las puertas o desplazarse sobre rieles; ello facilita el acceso hasta el fondo.

Une cuisine bien agencée doit exploiter au mieux l'espace disponible et toutes les possibilités doivent avoir été envisagées. Les ensembles modulaires vous permettent d'organiser votre cuisine et de choisir sa configuration. Si vos placards sont profonds, installez vos étagères sur des glissières de façon à ce qu'elles soient coulissantes pour pouvoir atteindre les objets qui se trouvent tout au fond.

Eine gut eingerichtete Küche nutzt geschickt alle zur Verfügung stehenden Winkel. Modularsysteme stellen eine Lösung dar, die das Design von Stauraum verschiedener Art ermöglichen. Wenn die Regale tief sind, können sie so gestaltet werden, dass sie beim Öffnen der Türen herausgezogen werden oder auf Schienen laufen. Dies erleichtert den Zugriff bis nach ganz hinten.

buffets
trinchadores
buffets
anrichten

THE BUFFET dates back to the Thirteenth Century, although it became more widely used in the latter half of the Nineteenth Century. Today it is one of the most valued auxiliary items of furniture in the dining room because of its huge range of shapes and guises; it can be put anywhere and is decorative; it can be used for keeping table service articles and is a good option when space is limited. When the living room and dining room share the same environment, the buffet can be used as a point of transition between the two spaces and will afford them personality and warmth.

EL TRINCHADOR tuvo su origen en el siglo XIII, aunque su uso se popularizó a partir de la segunda mitad de XIX. Hoy por hoy es uno de los muebles auxiliares de comedor más apreciados por su gran variedad de formas; porque facilita su integración en cualquier espacio y estilo decorativo; permite guardar las piezas del servicio de mesa y resuelve limitaciones de espacio. Cuando la sala y el comedor comparten el mismo ambiente, el trinchador puede utilizarse como una transición entre ambos espacios y dotarlos de personalidad y calidez.

LE BUFFET / VAISSELIER existe depuis le XIII siècle bien que son usage ne se soit répandu qu'à partir de la deuxième moitié du XIX. À l'heure actuelle, c'est l'un des meubles de salle à manger les plus appréciés en raison des formes variées qu'il peut prendre. Il s'adapte à n'importe quel espace et à tous les styles et permet de ranger le service de table et de résoudre de nombreux problèmes d'espace. Si vous avez par exemple un salon/salle à manger, ce meuble peut être utilisé pour diviser l'espace et lui apporter chaleur et personnalité.

DIE ANRICHTE hat ihren Ursprung im XIII. Jahrhundert, obwohl ihr Gebrauch erst ab der zweiten Hälfte des XIX. Jahrhunderts populär wurde. Heutzutage ist die Anrichte aufgrund der grossen Vielfalt an Formen eines der meistgeschätzten Möbel im Esszimmer, denn es kann an jedes Platzangebot und jede Stilrichtung angepasst werden. Eine Anrichte kann dazu dienen Teile des Service unterzubringen oder Platzprobleme zu beheben.
Wenn das Wohnzimmer und das Esszimmer sich in der gleichen Räumlichkeit befinden, kann die Anrichte zur Trennung der beiden Bereiche herangezogen werden und verleiht Persönlichkeit und Wärme.

The table or sideboard should be comprised of different-sized shelves with heights that can be graduated, as well as drawers with compartments for keeping table service items.

Conviene que el bufete o aparador se constituya de repisas de distintas proporciones cuya altura pueda graduarse, así como de cajones con compartimentos que permitan guardar lo necesario para el servicio de la mesa.

Pour pouvoir accueillir tout le service de table, il est préférable que le buffet possède des étagères de différentes dimensions et des tablettes réglables ainsi que des tiroirs divisés en compartiments.

Es ist angebracht, dass die Anrichte Regale mit verschiedenen Grössen aufweist, deren Höhe variiert werden kann. Ferner sollte sie Schubladen mit Fächern haben, in denen alles Notwendige zum Eindecken des Tisches verstaut werden kann.

While the buffet can be functional on the inside, the ideal thing would be for the outside to blend in with the other elements around it. Simple shapes and smooth finishes help tone down the dominance and volume of this piece of furniture in the dining room.

Si bien el trinchador debe contar con un interior funcional, es óptimo que externamente armonice con el resto de los elementos con los que convivirá. Las formas sencillas y los acabados lisos ayudan a aligerar el protagonismo y el volumen de este mueble en el área de comedor.

S'il est vrai que l'intérieur du buffet doit être fonctionnel, il n'en reste pas moins que son aspect extérieur doit s'harmoniser avec le reste du mobilier. Les formes dépouillées et les surfaces lisses permettent d'atténuer l'aspect massif de ce meuble ainsi que sa présence dans la salle à manger.

Auch wenn die Anrichte im Inneren funktionell sein soll, muss das Äussere dennoch mit dem Rest der Elemente in der Umgebung harmonisieren. Einfache Formen und glatte Oberflächen tragen dazu bei, die Geltung und den Umfang dieses Möbels im Bereich des Esszimmers zu verringern.

Horizontal sideboards are easy on the eye, as vertical ones may be heavier going, albeit with better storage options.

Los aparadores horizontales son ligeros a la vista, en tanto que los verticales pueden resultar pesados pero con mayores posibilidades de guardado.

Les buffets horizontaux sont moins lourds esthétiquement parlant que les vaisseliers qui ont en revanche de plus grandes capacités de rangement.

Waagerechte Anrichten sehen leichter aus, wohingegen senkrechte Anrichten schwerer wirken, aber mehr Möglichkeiten zum Aufbewahren bieten.

One of the contributions of contemporary Italian design
to tables with drawers is the blend of materials used; the
combination of wood, glass and aluminum lend this piece
of furniture an unusual sense of transparency, displaying
the contrast between materials in a very contemporary
esthetic context.

Una de las aportaciones del diseño italiano actual a la
cómoda bufete es la mezcla de materiales; la combinación
de madera, cristal y aluminio dotan a este mueble de
un inusual sentido de transparencia, permitiendo que se
perciba el contraste entre materiales, en una propuesta
estética muy contemporánea.

L'un des apports des designers italiens contemporains en ce
qui concerne les buffets est le mélange des matériaux. La
combinaison bois, verre et aluminium permet de donner à
ces meubles une transparence inhabituelle et de créer des
contrastes esthétiques très en vogue actuellement.

Einer der Beiträge des derzeitigen italienischen Designs im
Bereich der Anrichten, ist der Materialmix. Die Kombination
von Holz, Glas und Aluminium verleihem diesem Möbel eine
ungewöhnliche Transparenz und der Kontrast zwischen den
Materialien wird als eine sehr moderne und ästhetische
Lösung wahrgenommen.

The inside of this supporting furniture can be used for keeping both plates, cutlery, glasses and tablecloths as well as any food that needs to be kept close to the table; in both cases, the depth of this item is essential for its functions. If it has drawers then they should slide along metal runners, and the handles should be physically attractive, in proportion to the size of the drawers and balanced in accordance with their weight. Doors can have handles or closing systems that rely on magnets.

El interior de estos muebles de apoyo puede utilizarse tanto para el guardado de vajillas, cubertería, cristalería y mantelería como para alimentos que conviene tener próximos a la mesa; en ambos casos, la profundidad del mueble es esencial para su funcionalidad. Si cuenta con cajones es importante que éstos se desplacen por correderas metálicas, que sus jaladeras sean estéticas, proporcionales al tamaño de las gavetas y colocadas equilibradamente de acuerdo con su peso. En el caso de las puertas, éstas pueden utilizar jaladeras o un sistema de cerrado a presión imantado.

Le buffet peut abriter la vaisselle, les couverts, les verres et le linge de table mais aussi les denrées et condiments dont on a besoin tous les jours. La profondeur du meuble est donc essentielle. Si le buffet est équipé de tiroirs, il est important que ceux-ci soient à glissière, que les poignées soient adaptées à leurs dimensions et qu'elles soient agréables à regarder. En ce qui concerne les portes, celles-ci peuvent être munies de poignées ou de fermetures à pression aimantées.

Das Innere dieses Möbels kann zur Aufbewahrung von Geschirr, Besteck, Gläsern und Tischdecken genutzt werden, sowie auch von Nahrungsmitteln, die sich in der Nähe des Tisches befinden sollten. In beiden Fällen ist für die Zweckmässigkeit die Tiefe des Möbels ausschlaggebend. Wenn Schubladen vorhanden sind, ist es wichtig, dass diese auf Metallschienen laufen, ihre Griffe ästhetisch sind, ihre Grösse im Verhältnis zu den Schubladen steht und sie in Übereinstimmung mit ihrem Gewicht angebracht werden. Die Türen können über Griffe oder ein Schliesssystem auf Magnetbasis verfügen.

living areas
zonas de estar
pièces à vivre
wohnräume

studios
estudios
bureaux
arbeitsräume

THE PROBLEM OF STORAGE in living areas is complicated by the fact that they are the most vital areas of the home and are where a large proportion of work activities are performed and time is spent together with others. It is still possible, however, to obtain a clear environment by designing storage furniture in accordance with the type and pace of activities of the inhabitants. If the home does not have a study, a feasible option would be to keep the computer or an item of furniture on wheels that serves as a work table in one of the corners.

EL PROBLEMA DE GUARDADO en las zonas de estar es complicado, debido a que éstas son las áreas más vitales de la casa y donde se realizan gran parte de las actividades de trabajo y convivencia. Sin embargo, es posible lograr ambientes despejados si se diseña el mobiliario de guardado en función del tipo y el ritmo de actividad de sus habitantes. Cuando se carece de un estudio es factible usar una esquina para colocar la computadora o algún mueble de almacenaje con ruedas que haga las veces de mesa de trabajo.

LE PROBLEME DU RANGEMENT est plus compliqué à résoudre quand il s'agit des salles de séjour qui sont le centre vital d'un logement : on y travaille, on y accueille la famille et les amis. On peut toutefois parvenir à dégager l'espace à condition de choisir des meubles de rangement adaptés aux activités et au rythme de vie de la maison. Si vous ne disposez pas d'une pièce pouvant servir de bureau, vous pouvez aménager un coin du salon où vous disposerez votre ordinateur sur un meuble monté sur roulettes faisant à la fois office de table de travail.

DAS PROBLEM DES AUFBEWAHRENS in den Wohnbereichen ist kompliziert, weil es sich hierbei um die wichtigsten Räume des Hauses handelt, in denen ein grosser Teil der Arbeit und des Zusammenseins stattfinden. Dennoch ist es möglich, eine unbeschwerte Atmosphäre zu schaffen, wenn die Stauräume in Übereinstimmung mit der Art und dem Rhythmus der Tätigkeiten der Bewohner gestaltet werden. Wenn kein Arbeitszimmer vorhanden ist, kann eine Ecke dazu genuzt werden, dort einen Computer zu installieren oder ein Möbel mit Rädern aufzustellen, das sowohl zum Verstauen von Gegenständen als auch als Arbeitstisch genutzt werden kann.

CREATING STORAGE SPACE that did not exist before is essential in a study. The best option of stationery is drawers or a filing system either under or next to the desk. Choosing multi-function storage furniture and placing it in the perimeter of the room is also very useful and helps keep order. Similarly, making the most of the depth of sofas and work tables through pull-out drawers helps optimize space and is ideal for storing stationery in bulk as well as other items that are not used very often.

CREAR ESPACIO DE ALMACENAJE que no existía e esencial en un estudio. Para la papelería convien tener una cajonera-archivero preferentemente deba del escritorio o a un costado de éste. Elegir muebles d guardado multifunción y colocarlos en el perímetro d cuarto es también de gran utilidad y ayuda a manten el orden. Asimismo, aprovechar la profundidad d sofás y mesas de trabajo mediante cajones extraíble coopera al rendimiento del espacio y se presta par almacenar artículos de papelería comprados e cantidad y otro tipo de objetos que no son utilizad habitualmente.

CRÉER UN ESPACE DE RANGEMENT qui n'existait pas dans votre bureau est essentiel. Pour ranger vos papiers, la meilleure solution est le caisson à tiroirs (dont un tiroir classeur pour vos dossiers) qui sera placé de préférence sous la table de travail ou à côté. Vous pouvez aussi choisir des meubles de rangement multifonctionnels et les placer le long des murs. Pour gagner de la place, pensez également à exploiter la profondeur des canapés ou des tables de travail en les équipant de tiroirs coulissants où vous pourrez stocker vos réserves de papier et les objets que vous utilisez rarement.

DAS SCHAFFEN VON STAURAUM, der vorher nicht vorhanden war, ist unerlässlich in einen Arbeitsraum. Für Schreibwaren ist es angebracht, eine Schubladenschrank unter oder neben dem Schreibtisch aufzustellen. Die Auswahl von multifunktionellen Aktenschränken und deren Aufstellung im Raum ist sehr nützlich und hilft dabei, Ordnung zu halten. Ferner kann die Tiefe von Sofas und Arbeitstischen genutzt werden, indem ausziehbare Schubladen angebracht werden, die den Stauraum vergrössern. Dort können Schreibwaren untergebracht werden, die in grossen Mengen angeschafft wurden oder andere Objekte, die nicht sehr häufig gebraucht werden.

Whatever the style may be, in order to understand the importance of workspace-arranging furniture in the home today, it is necessary to bear in mind that we are dealing with a simple ordering of equipment, a desk and a seat, to turn it into a truly interactive place where information is processed. This circumstance transforms the organizer into a very personal item of furniture in the context of the home that, unlike the TV, requires the placing of the computer, monitor, keyboard and space for keeping digital back-ups.

Sea cual sea el estilo, para comprender la importancia que tiene hoy el mueble organizador en los espacios de trabajo del hogar es necesario tener en cuenta que estos últimos han pasado de ser una simple agrupación de equipo, escritorio y silla, para convertirse en verdaderos lugares interactivos donde se procesa información. Esta circunstancia transforma al organizador en un mueble muy personal dentro del contexto de la vivienda, que a cambio de la televisión demanda la ubicación de la computadora, monitor, teclado y espacio para resguardar respaldos digitales.

Quel que soit leur style, les postes de travail prennent une importance croissante dans nos foyers ; ces meubles qui n'étaient auparavant qu'un assemblage - table, chaise et matériel informatique - sont devenus de véritables espaces interactifs destinés au traitement de l'information. Au contraire du meuble TV, le poste de travail devient donc un meuble très personnel dans le contexte du logement et doit avoir la capacité d'accueillir un ordinateur (unité centrale, écran et clavier) et disposer d'un espace permettant de classer les CD et autres supports numériques.

Ganz gleichgültig welcher Stil bevorzugt wird: um die Wichtigkeit von Organisationsmöbeln im Arbeitsbereich eines Wohnhauses zu verstehen, muss man in Betracht ziehen, dass es sich nicht mehr nur eine Anordnung von Ausrüstung, Schreibtisch und Stuhl handelt, sondern um einen interaktiven Bereich, in dem Information verarbeitet wird. Dieser Umstand verwandelt den Büroschrank in ein sehr persönliches Möbel, das sich der Umgebung des Wohnraumes anpasst und-im Gegensatz zum Fernsehen- das Aufstellen eines Computers, eines Monitors, einer Tastatur und von Stauraum zum Aufbewahren von digitaler Information erforderlich macht.

tv rooms
salas de televisión
salles de tv
fernsehzimmer

THE SET OF ITEMS in a TV room does not stand out for its esthetic flow. This is why it is a good idea to take the spotlight off the products themselves and generate simple environments that imitate the context of the home. Mimicry is achieved with very slim artifacts and furniture characterized by simple lines. Glass doors and covers are also ideal for this, as is the inclusion of carpentry work whose design corresponds to the setting of the home and helps tone down the particular features of the appliances.

EL CONJUNTO DE ELEMENTOS en un cuarto de televisión no se destaca precisamente por su continuidad estética. Por esta razón, conviene dejar atrás el show de los productos y generar ambientes simples que busquen imitar el contexto de la casa. La mimetización se logra a través de aparatos muy delgados y mobiliario de líneas sencillas. Son asimismo idóneas las cubiertas y puertas de vidrio e la incorporación de un trabajo de carpintería cuyo diseño esté acorde con el entorno del hogar y permite disimular los rasgos particulares de los equipos.

ES ÉLÉMENTS qui composent habituellement ameublement d'une salle de TV laissent souvent à ésirer quant à leurs qualités esthétiques. Il convient onc de ne pas se laisser séduire par l'étalage des roduits existants sur le marché et de préférer un meublement conforme au style du reste de la naison. Si vous avez des appareils plats aux lignes ures, choisissez des meubles munis de portes en verre dans le cas contraire, dissimulez-les dans des meubles n bois encastrés que vous adapterez selon vos goûts t votre style.

DIE ELEMENTE in einem Fernsehzimmer heben sich nicht gerade durch ihre ästhetische Gleichförmigkeit ab. Daher ist es angebracht, die Produktshow in den Hintergrund zu stellen und eine einfache Atmosphäre zu schaffen, die dem Gesamteindruck des Hauses entspricht. Die Integration in die Umgebung wird durch sehr dünne Geräte und Möbel mit klaren Linien erzielt. Gleichermassen geeignet sind Glasabdeckungen und -türen oder ein extra angefertigtes Möbelstück, das in Bezug auf sein Design mit der übrigen Wohnung übereinstimmt und die Ausrüstungen verbirgt.

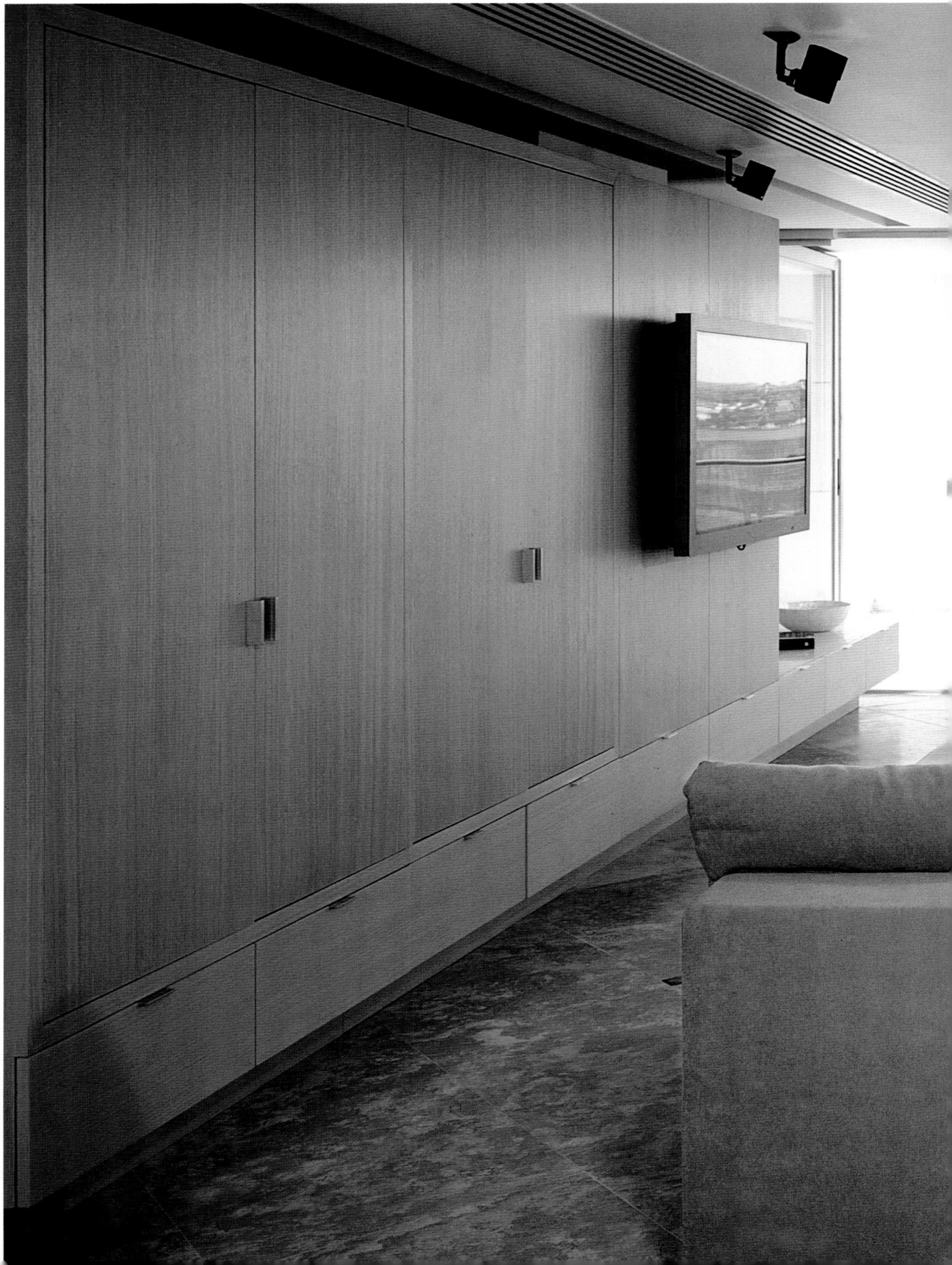

Modular divisions for making shelves are very useful in TV rooms, as they allow electronic appliances - also created as modular systems - to be suitably arranged.

Las divisiones modulares para formar estanterías son muy útiles en las salas de televisión, pues permiten el ordenamiento de los aparatos electrónicos que también son creados como sistemas modulares.

Les tablettes réglables permettant de créer des niveaux et des compartiments sont utiles dans une salle de TV afin de mieux ranger les appareils électroniques qui sont également conçus comme des ensembles modulaires.

Module zur Bildung von Regalen sind sehr nützlich in Fernsehzimmern, da sie es ermöglichen, elektronische Geräte ordentlich unterzubringen, die ebenfalls aus modulen Systemen bestehen.

Small wardrobes help hide electronic appliances and essential cables. But the slender design and appearance of some appliances mean they can be displayed in some cases. This applies for TV sets and speakers that combine with the warmth of wood to highlight their cutting edge status.

Los pequeños armarios ayudan a ocultar equipos electrónicos y cables indispensables para su funcionamiento. Pero es permisible que por su grácil diseño y materialidad algunos aparatos sean exhibidos; es el caso de televisiones y bocinas que mezclados con la calidez de la madera acentúan su condición vanguardista.

Vous pouvez dissimuler les appareils électroniques et les câbles indispensables à leur fonctionnement dans de petits placards ou caissons. Les appareils au design soigné et élégant (écran plat, enceintes) peuvent toutefois rester visibles ; par contraste, leurs lignes contemporaines mettront en valeur la chaleur du bois.

Kleine Schränke helfen dabei, Elektrogeräte sowie für das Funktionieren notwendige Kabel zu verbergen. Einige Geräte können auch aufgrund ihres formschönen Designs und ansprechenden Materials zur Schau gestellt werden. Dabei handelt es sich um Fernseher und Lautsprecherboxen, die in Verbindung mit der Wärme des Holzes avantgardistisch aussehen.

Given its volume, the sofa is a key element, and a good option is to surround it by low visual impact furniture with a lot of storage space.

Dado su volumen, el sofá es una pieza clave, por lo que conviene acompañarlo de muebles de poco peso visual, pero con mucho espacio para almacenar.

Le canapé, en raison de son volume, est l'élément principal de la pièce ; il doit donc être accompagné de meubles discrets au niveau visuel mais disposant d'une grande capacité de rangement.

Aufgrund seines Umfanges ist das Sofa das zentrale Möbelstück und sollte durch visuell leichte Möbel umgeben sein, die aber gleichzeitig auch viel Stauraum bieten.

The entertainment center is an ad hoc item of furniture for the TV room, as it facilitates the installation of the more common audiovisual appliances. Nonetheless, even though it is a traditional alternative in which it is worth considering storage space, it is not the only solution. One very tasteful alternative consists of placing wooden panels with loose panel and low lights, installed on a wooden base of the same tone, at symmetric heights and equidistant from the sleek plasma screen TV set.

El centro de entretenimiento es un mueble ad hoc para la sala de televisión, ya que facilita la instalación de los aparatos audiovisuales más comunes. No obstante, pese a que se trata de una alternativa tradicional que vale la pena considerar dentro de los espacios para almacenaje, no es la única solución. Una opción altamente decorativa consiste en la colocación de entrepaños de madera con lambrín suelto y luz inferior, instalados sobre una base de madera del mismo tono a alturas simétricas y equidistantes de una esbelta televisión con pantalla de plasma.

Le meuble TV et Hi-fi est conçu spécialement pour les salles de TV et étudié pour contenir les appareils audiovisuels les plus courants. Il constitue certes une solution pratique en raison de sa capacité de rangement mais ce n'est pas la seule. Un assemblage de panneaux lambrissés flottants équidistants, disposés à différents niveaux autour d'un bel écran plasma, monté sur un socle en bois de même couleur et éclairé par le bas constitue une option bien plus décorative.

Ein Fernsehmöbel ist ein ad hoc-Element für das Fernsehzimmer, da in ihm die gebräuchlichsten audiovisuellen Geräte untergebracht werden können. Dennoch handelt es sich dabei nicht um die einzige, wohl aber eine traditionelle Lösung, die auch Stauraum bietet. Eine äusserst dekorative Alternative stellen Regalbretter mit Unterlicht dar, die auf einer Holzbasis der gleichen Farbe und auf gleicher Höhe sowie in gleichem Abstand von einem Plasma-Flachbildfernseher angebracht werden.

THE BOOKSHELF is a piece of furniture created to fit into a given space and keep books arranged in a specific order within the interior decoration of the library, which makes it all the easier to consult them. Design solutions vary depending on the owner's preferences, but books can also be interspersed with decorative objects on different sized niches on peripheral items of furniture, accomplishing the dual objective of function and look.

EL LIBRERO es un mueble creado para acomodar en un espacio determinado y con un orden específico los libros dentro de la decoración interior de la biblioteca, con el valor añadido de facilitar la manera de utilizarlos y su consulta. Las soluciones de su diseño varían según las preferencias del dueño pero, desde luego, a través de muebles periféricos on diversidad de tamaños de nichos es factible alternar el acomodo de os volúmenes con objetos decorativos, logrando el doble objetivo de la unción y la estética.

A BIBLIOTHÉQUE est un meuble créé pour ranger et classer des livres dans n espace déterminé. Ce meuble doit s'adapter à la décoration de la ièce faisant office de salle de lecture et permettre une consultation apide de son contenu. Les designers ont imaginé toutes sortes de solutions onvenant aux goûts variés des consommateurs ; la division du meuble n compartiments de toutes dimensions permet d'alterner livres et objets écoratifs et de marier ainsi fonctionnalité et esthétique.

DAS REGAL ist ein Möbelstück, das dazu dient auf einem bestimmten Raum und mit einer bestimmten Ordnung im Rahmen der Innendekoration der Bibliothek ücher unterzubringen. Dabei wird der zusätzliche Nutzen erzielt, dass die Art und Weise die Bücher zu benutzen und darin nachzuschlagen erleichtert wird. Die Lösungen in Bezug auf das Design hängen von den Vorlieben der Besitzer ab. Und natürlich können auch auf umgebenden Möbeln mit unterschiedlich grossen Fächern dekorative Objekte verschiedener Grösse aufgestellt werden, o dass Funktionalität und Ästhetik zugleich erzielt werden.

book shelves
libreros
bibliothèques
bibliotheken

The purpose of book shelves is to provide modulated spaces as a basis for arranging books. Depending on their style, they may vary in terms of shapes, colors and materials, but as far as size is concerned, full use must be made of any available space between the floor and ceiling, including double elevations, any problems of access being remedied by steps. Specific requirements will dictate whether shelf-only furniture or furniture with drawers within easy reach is chosen.

Las bases y el objetivo de las bibliotecas son servir de soporte para organizar los libros a través de espacios modulados. De acuerdo con su estilo pueden variar en formas, colores y materiales, pero en lo que respecta a su tamaño conviene aprovechar el espacio de piso a techo con el que se cuente, incluyendo las dobles alturas, pues para llegar hasta la ubicación de los libros existen escaleras. Con base en los requerimientos particulares se puede optar entre muebles que posean solo estantes o los que también incluyan cajones al alcance de la mano.

Une bibliothèque est conçue pour organiser une collection de livres dans un espace modulé. Selon vos goûts personnels, vous pouvez choisir entre les formes, les couleurs et les matériaux disponibles ; en revanche, pour ce qui est des dimensions de votre bibliothèque, pensez à tirer parti de l'espace compris entre le sol et le plafond, quitte à utiliser un escabeau si nécessaire. Suivant vos besoins particuliers, vous pouvez choisir une étagère simple ou une combinaison de caissons et d'étagères.

Der grundlegende Zweck von Bibliotheken ist die Organisation von Büchern durch modulare Systeme. In Übereinstimmung mit dem jeweiligen Stil können die Formen, Farben und Materialien variieren, aber in Bezug auf die Grösse ist es angebracht, den vorhandenen Platz vom Boden bis zur Decke zu nutzen. Dabei können auch doppelte Deckenhöhen genutzt werden, denn das Zugangsproblem kann durch eine Leiter gelöst werden. Auf der Grundlage der jeweiligen Erfordernisse können Möbel gewählt werden, die nur über Regalbretter verfügen oder solche, die auf Handhöhe auch Schubladen aufweisen.

Contemporary design allows us to experiment with original details in bookshelves, such as arranging them without any side views leaving edges jutting out or shelves without vertical supports, or when they are designed to be held in place by turnbuckles. The placing of the panels can be adjusted, in terms of both height and width, to afford the shelves even more mobility, and objects with different shapes, visual intensity and materials can be put on them and alternated with the books.

El diseño contemporáneo permite experimentar con detalles originales en los libreros, como ocurre al realizarlos sin vistas laterales dejando los bordes en voladizo o las repisas sin sostenes verticales, o bien cuando se les concibe para ser sujetados por medio de tensores. Mayor movimiento aún puede adquirir una estantería si se juega con la disposición de los entrepaños tanto en su altura como en su anchura, y se colocan sobre ellos objetos con diferentes formas, pesos visuales y de distinta materialidad, alternándolos con el acomodo de los libros.

es designers actuels tentent d'apporter des détails originaux aux bibliothèques. On trouve ainsi des étagères sans
anneaux latéraux, des étagères flottantes, des étagères sans support verticaux ou des étagères suspendues par des
âbles tenseurs. Il est aussi possible de donner plus de mouvement au système d'étagères en jouant avec la disposition des
anneaux tant au niveau de la hauteur que de la profondeur ou en y plaçant des objets de formes et de matériaux variés
ont la présence visuelle contrastera avec celle des livres.

as moderne Design von Bücherregalen ermöglicht ein Experimentieren mit originellen Details, wie zum Beispiel ein Verzicht
uf die Seitenansicht, so dass die Ränder aus Vorsprüngen bestehen oder Regalbretter ohne waagerechte Stützen, so dass
e Bücher durch Spanner gehalten werden. Ein Bücherregal wird auch interessanter, wenn in Bezug auf die Höhe und auch
uf die Breite mit der Anordnung der Regalbretter gespielt wird und darauf dann Objekte mit unterschiedlicher Form, visuellem
ewicht und aus verschiedenen Materialien gestellt werden. Diese werden dann abwechselnd mit Büchern kombiniert.

The current trend in library design favors simple and straight shapes; these help graduate the heights of shelves, making sure the furniture is used in a more versatile manner without undermining its practical usefulness.

La tendencia actual en el diseño de bibliotecas es hacia las formas simples y rectas; éstas facilitan la graduación de las alturas de las repisas, logrando que el mueble sea utilizado de forma más variada y sin que por ello pierda su carácter utilitario.

La tendance actuelle du design en ce qui concerne les bibliothèques est aux formes simples et rectilignes ; ce type de design permet d'avoir des étagères réglables et de donner différents usages à ce meuble sans qu'il perde son caractère utilitaire.

Die derzeitige Tendenz in Bezug auf das Design von Bibliotheken geht zu einfachen und geraden Formen, die die Abstufung der Regalbretterhöhe erleichtern. So kann das Möbel auf vielfältigere Weise genutzt werden und verliert dennoch nicht seinen Nutzcharakter.

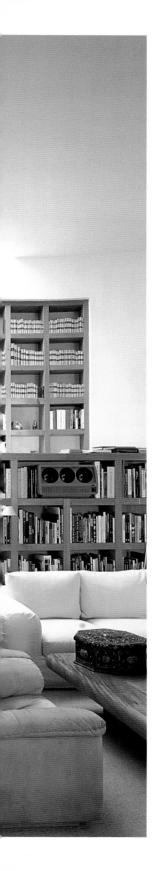

The appeal of an item of furniture for keeping books can be mimicked by architecture, especially if it is curved. But if the width, height and load are huge, its structure must be designed so that the shelves can hold the weight and the supporting posts are proportional to this weight.

Es atractivo que un mueble para resguardar libros se mimetice con la arquitectura, sobre todo si ésta es curva. Pero si además el ancho, el alto y la carga son colosales, su cálculo estructural debe diseñarse para que las repisas soporten y los postes de contención sean proporcionales al peso que reciban.

Il est bon qu'une bibliothèque puisse s'adapter à l'architecture qui l'environne surtout quand celle-ci est marquée par les lignes courbes. Si la profondeur, la hauteur et la charge que devra supporter le meuble sont importantes, veillez à effectuer les calculs structurels nécessaires et à choisir les poutres servant de support à l'ensemble en fonction du poids à supporter.

Es ist attraktiv, wenn ein Möbel zum Aufbewahren von Büchern sich in die Architektur einfügt, vor allem wenn es auch den Kurven folgt. Wenn aber ausserdem die Breite, die Höhe und die Belastung gewaltig sind, muss eine Strukturberechnung durchgeführt werden, damit die Regalbretter standhalten und die Stützpfosten proportional zum jeweiligen Gewicht gestaltet werden.

Ground glass sliding doors help economize on space, and can provide surprising esthetic effects on shelves when combined with the optical plays of panels. However, it is important for the ironworks and fastening system of the runners to be safe and easy to use.

Las puertas corredizas de vidrio esmerilado ayudan a economizar espacio y combinadas con los juegos reticulares de entrepaños ofrecen efectos estéticos sorprendentes en una estantería. Sin embargo, es importante que el sistema de herrajes y sujeción de las correderas sea seguro y de fácil manipulación.

Les portes en verre coulissantes permettent, tout en faisant des économies d'espace, d'obtenir des effets esthétiques surprenants, surtout quand elles s'ajoutent à un réseau de panneaux. Veillez cependant à ce que le système de fermeture, de fixation et de glissières soit sûr et facile à manipuler.

Schiebetüren aus geschliffenem Glas helfen Platz zu sparen. Und kombiniert mit netzartig angebrachten Regalbrettern bieten sie ferner einen überraschend ästhetischen Anblick. Dabei ist es wichtig, dass die Beschläge und die Aufhängung der Schiebevorrichtung sicher und leicht zu handhaben sind.

bathrooms & bedrooms

baños y recámaras

chambres et salles de bains

schlafzimmer und badezimmer

bureaus and chests of drawers
buroes y cajoneras
tables de nuits et commodes
nachtschränke und kommoden

CHESTS OF DRAWERS have made their way back into contemporary decoration with the same structure and functions as before, but now looking more modern and stylish thanks to the simplicity of their shapes, the sobriety of their ornamental value and the novel methods and materials used to make them, such as glass and steel. This furniture is functional and is designed to optimize architectural space and provide the best useful area possible for keeping things in, as well as comfort in the bedroom.

LAS CÓMODAS Y CAJONERAS han vuelto a la decoración actual con la misma estructura y función que solían tener antaño, pero gracias a la simplicidad de sus formas, a la sobriedad de su decorado y a las novedosas técnicas y materiales con los que se fabrican, como el vidrio o el acero, su aspecto resulta moderno y elegante. Son muebles funcionales diseñados para optimizar el espacio arquitectónico y brindar la mayor área útil posible para guardado, ofreciendo comodidad dentro de la habitación.

LES COMMODES sont de retour dans le monde de la décoration; elles possèdent la même structure et les mêmes fonctions qu'autrefois mais leur aspect a changé : grâce à la simplicité des formes, à la sobriété des ornements, à l'innovation technique et à l'emploi de matériaux tels que le verre et l'acier, ce sont à présent des meubles fonctionnels au design élégant et contemporain, conçus à la fois pour tirer au mieux parti de l'espace architectural et pour apporter une touche de confort dans votre chambre à coucher.

KOMMODEN UND SCHRÄNKE MIT SCHUBFÄCHERN sind wieder zur derzeitigen Dekoration zurückgekehrt, und dies mit derselben Struktur und Funktionsweise wie einst. Aber dank der einfachen Formen, wenig Dekoration und neuen Techniken und Materialien mit denen sie hergestellt werden, wie Glas und Stahl, sind sie dennoch modern und elegant. Es handelt sich um funktionelle Möbel, die zur Optimierung des architektonischen Raumes hergestellt werden. Sie bieten den grösstmöglichen Stauraum und sind ausserdem sehr bequem.

In the Nineteenth Century, wardrobes and chests of drawers began to lose their decorative role and became merely functional items for keeping clothes in. However, since the mid-Twentieth Century, the emergence of the sliding door closet and the dressing room as a complement to the bedroom meant that this furniture fell into disuse. Wardrobes are tall and have doors and shelves, while their physical and esthetic features make them ideal for concealing electrical appliances in the bedroom. Chests of drawers are items of furniture with a flat surface and drawers, and they are still used for keeping clothes, albeit with a decorative dimension.

En el siglo XIX los armarios y las cómodas perdieron su calidad decorativa, convirtiéndose en piezas funcionales para guardar ropa. Sin embargo, desde mediados del siglo XX, con la integración del clóset de puertas corredizas y el vestidor como complemento de la habitación, estos muebles entraron en desuso. Los armarios son altos y tienen puertas y estantes, sus características físicas y estéticas los hacen idóneos para ocultar aparatos electrónicos en las recámaras. Las cómodas son muebles con tablero de mesa y cajoneras, aún se usan como guardarropas pero también como elementos decorativos.

Les armoires et commodes ont perdu leurs qualités décoratives au XIX siècle pour devenir des meubles fonctionnels destinés au rangement des vêtements. Vers le milieu du XX siècle, ces meubles sont tombés en désuétude et ont été remplacés dans les chambres à coucher par le placard à portes coulissantes et le dressing. À l'heure actuelle, les armoires étant des meubles hauts, munis de portes et d'étagères, elles sont parfaites pour dissimuler les appareils électroniques qu'on trouve parfois dans les chambres. Les commodes sont munies de tiroirs et d'un dessus ; on s'en sert encore pour ranger des vêtements mais aussi en tant que meuble purement décoratif.

Im XIX. Jahrhundert haben die Schränke und Kommoden ihren dekorativen Wert verloren und sich in funktionelle Möbel zum Aufbewahren von Kleidung verwandelt. Dennoch sind sie seit Mitte des XX. Jahrhunderts aus dem Gebrauch gekommen und durch Kleiderschränke mit Schiebetüren und Ankleideräume als Bestandteil der Räume ersetzt worden. Kleiderschränke sind hoch und verfügen über Türen und Regale. Aufgrund ihrer physischen und ästhetischen Eigenschaften sind sie auch zum Verstauen von elektronischen Geräten in Schlafzimmern geeignet. Kommoden sind Möbel mit einer Ablagefläche und Schubladen. Sie werden sowohl zum Aufbewahren von Kleidung als auch zur Dekoration benutzt.

The bed is the focal point of the bedroom, but the bureaus are no less important, given that they accompany the headboards. The bureau is a small piece of furniture with drawers, and its purpose is to keep things that are essential before sleeping, during the night and on waking up. This is why it should be safe, without any sharp corners and with shallow drawers. But just because it is a functional element, there is no reason why it should not also make an esthetic contribution, especially as its location next to the centerpiece of the bedroom means it will never go unnoticed.

La cama es el punto focal de una recámara, pero los burós no son menos relevantes, toda vez que acompañan a las cabeceras. El buró es un mueble pequeño, con cajones, que sirve para guardar las cosas que serán indispensables antes de dormir, durante la noche y al despertar. Por ello conviene que sea seguro, que sus esquinas no sean agresivas y que sus cajones sean poco profundos. Pero no por ser parte del mobiliario funcional debe carecer de estética pues, dado que está junto al mueble principal, siempre llamará la atención.

lit est le centre de la chambre à coucher ; les tables de nuit n'en restent pas moins importantes puisqu'elles complètent tête de lit. La table de nuit est un petit meuble muni de tiroirs où l'on peut ranger les objets indispensables avant de endormir, pendant la nuit ou au réveil. Choisissez de préférence des meubles sûrs, aux angles arrondis, munis de tiroirs eu profonds. Bien que fonctionnelles, les tables de nuit ne doivent pas pour autant être privées de qualités esthétiques car omme elles se trouvent à côté du meuble principal, elles attireront forcément le regard.

as Bett ist der Mitterpunkt eines Schlafzimmers, aber auch die Nachtschränke sind nicht weniger relevant, da sie einen il des Kopfendes bilden. Der Nachtschrank ist ein kleines Möbel mit Schubladen zum Aufbewahren von Dingen, die vor em Schlafen, in der Nacht oder am Morgen benutzt werden. Daher ist es angebracht, dass es sich um ein sicheres Möbel andelt, ohne aggressive Ecken und mit nicht sehr tiefen Schubladen. Aber aufgrund der Tatsache, dass es sich um einen l der funktionellen Möbel handelt, muss trotzdem nicht auf Ästhetik verzichtet werden. Denn da es neben dem Hauptmöbel eht, wird es immer die Blicke auf sich ziehen.

One good option is to use the bedroom walls to increase storage space, but this may have a negative visual effect. To keep the volume down, it is advisable to use shelves without doors, and niches.

Utilizar los muros de una recámara para incrementar el espacio de almacenaje es una solución válida pero puede resultar visualmente denso, para restar volumen se recomiendan los estantes sin puertas, y las oquedades.

es murs peuvent vous fournir une solution si vous avez besoin d'espace de rangement dans une chambre à condition d'éviter de surcharger l'aspect de la pièce. Choisissez des étagères sans portes ou aménagez des cavités.

Die Benutzung der Wände eines Schafzimmers, um den Stauraum zu vergrössern, ist eine Möglichkeit, kann aber visuell schwer wirken. Um das Volumen zu verringern, sind Regale ohne Türen und Hohlräume empfehlenswert.

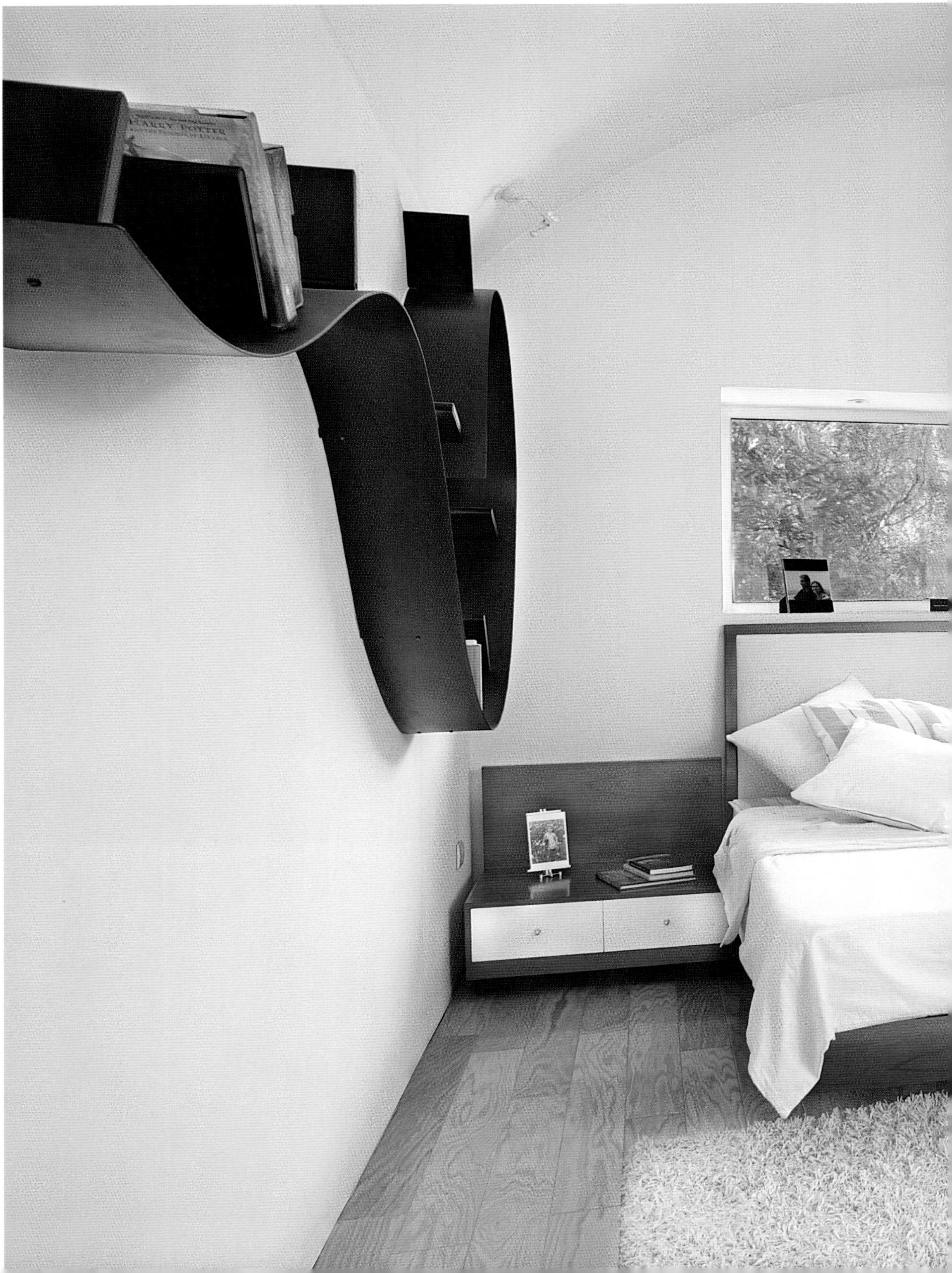
HARRY POTTER

Storage furniture for children must be visually attractive and practical, and as resilient as it is safe. Closets, chests of drawers, toy chests and trunks should preferably be child size, allow children to experiment with them using all their senses, be easy to use, encourage active exploration and form part of their games. Their design should allow for easy access and be free of any sharp angles or other hazards, as early childhood is a time of avid investigation.

El mobiliario de guardado para niños debe ser tan estético como práctico y tan resistente como seguro. Conviene que clósets, cómodas, cajoneras, jugueteros y baúles se adecuen a la escala infantil, permitan que el niño pueda experimentar con ellos con todos sus sentidos, sean de manipulación sencilla, estimulen su exploración activa y que sus elementos formen parte del juego. Asimismo, su diseño debe contemplar el fácil acceso y estar libre de ángulos filosos y de otros riesgos, pues con la primera infancia llega también el tiempo de la investigación.

es meubles de rangement destinés à équiper une chambre d'enfant doivent être résistants, pratiques, sûrs et agréables à ·eil. Les placards, les commodes, les caissons, bahuts et autres coffres à jouets doivent être adaptés à la taille de l'enfant · stimuler ses sens et sa curiosité. Ils doivent être simples à utiliser et constituer un ensemble cohérent. Choisir des meubles ·ciles d'accès aux angles arrondis pour éviter tout risque de blessure ; n'oublions pas que la petite enfance, c'est aussi le ·mps de l'exploration.

·chränke für Kinder müssen genauso ästhetisch wie praktisch und genauso widerstandsfähig wie sicher sein. Es ist ·ngebracht die Kleiderschränke, Kommoden, Schubladenschränke, Spielzeugkisten und Truhen an den kindlichen Massstab ·zupassen, damit es dem Kind möglich ist, diese mit den Sinnen zu erfassen. Sie sollten einfach zu handhaben sein, die ·tive Erkundung stimulieren und die Elemente sollten spielerisch sein. Ausserdem sollte das Design einen einfachen Zugriff ·möglichen und keine scharfen Ecken oder andere Risiken aufweisen, denn Kinder erforschen gerne alles.

Multifunctional furniture is useful in children's bedrooms. A drawer can be used to store things, as well as double up as a toy box. Pull-out drawers under the bed can also be used for keeping large objects. Whatever their function, drawers should be spacious and allow a child to define order with a certain disorder; in other words, they should allow children to put things away quickly so they don't take for ever to tidy up their room.

Los muebles multifunción son una ayuda en cuartos infantiles. Un cajón puede servir para almacenar cosas y cumplir al mismo tiempo con la función de juguetero. También pueden usarse cajoneras extraíbles debajo de la cama para guardar grandes objetos. En todos los casos los cajones deben ser amplios y permitir que el niño mantenga, a través de ellos, un orden con cierto desorden; es decir, conviene que se basen en un sistema de guardado rápido para que no le tome mucho tiempo recoger su habitación.

meubles multifonctionnels sont très utiles dans les chambres d'enfants. Un caisson peut aussi bien servir de rangement
e de coffre à jouets. On peut encore placer des tiroirs coulissants sous le lit pour y ranger les objets les plus volumineux. Il
en tous les cas préférable de choisir des caissons et des tiroirs de grandes dimensions afin que l'enfant puisse y entasser
objets et donner un semblant d'ordre à sa chambre sans que cela soit trop long ou laborieux.

Itifunktionelle Möbel sind von grossem Wert in Kinderzimmern. Eine Schublade kann dazu dienen, Dinge aufzubewahren
d gleichzeitig auch als Spielzeugkiste benutzt werden. Es können auch Schubfächer unter dem Bett zum Aufbewahren
n grossen Objekten verwendet werden. Auf jeden Fall sollten die Schubladen gross sein und dem Kind ermöglichen, eine
wisse Ordnung zu halten, das heisst, es ist angebracht ein System zum schnellen Aufbewahren anzuwenden, damit nicht
Zeit darauf geht, das Zimmer aufzuräumen.

A SPACE for different sized objects allows us to use each and every corner of the closet or dressing room to the full. If we rationalize space and put everything in its place, we can even increase storage capacity. Boxes, shelves, racks, bars, hangers, hooks, tie racks and organizers, specially designed to bring order to an endless array of items and accessories that need to be put away, are but a few options for doing so. Organizers are particularly useful for using any lost or unused vertical space.

dressing rooms
vestidores
dressings
ankleidezimmer

CONTAR CON UN ESPACIO para los diversos tamaños de los objetos permite aprovechar al máximo cada rincón del clóset o del vestidor. Si se racionaliza el espacio y se coloca todo en su lugar, es posible acrecentar la capacidad de almacenamiento. Cajas, cajones, repisas, estanterías, barras, ganchos, colgaderas, corbateros y organizadores especialmente diseñados para cumplir la función de mantener en orden la infinidad de elementos y accesorios que es necesario guardar, son solamente algunas opciones para lograrlo, particularmente los organizadores ayudan a utilizar el espacio vertical perdido o desaprovechado.

DISPOSER D'UN ESPACE adapté aux différentes dimensions des objets permet de tirer parti au maximum de chaque recoin des placards ou du dressing. La division rationnelle de l'espace et l'ordre méthodique permettent d'accroître les capacités de rangement. Caissons, tiroirs, étagères, tablettes, penderies, crochets, porte-cravates et autres ne sont que quelques exemples d'aménagements intérieurs qui vous permettront de mettre de l'ordre dans vos vêtements et accessoires ; choisissez de préférence les aménagements intérieurs qui vous aideront à tirer parti de l'espace vertical souvent perdu ou mal employé.

WENN RAUM FÜR OBJEKTE verschiedener Grösse vorhanden ist ermöglicht dies, jeden Winkel des Schrankes oder Ankleideraumes optimal zu nutzen. Wenn der Raum geschickt eingeteilt und alles auf seinem Platz aufbewahrt wird, kann der Stauraum noch vergrössert werden. Kisten, Schubladen, Regalbretter, Borde, Stangen, Haken, Hängevorrichtungen, Krawattenhalter und Organizer, die speziell zur Erfüllung einer bestimmten Funktion hergestellt wurden, helfen dabei die vielen Elemente und Accesoires ordentlich unterzubringen. Besonders die Organizer sind dazu geeignet, waagerechten Raum zugänglich zu machen, der ohne sie nicht genutzt werden konnte.

ANY LONG GARMENTS AND PANTS that hang full-length require units 5 feet tall; for shirts and folded pants, the racks must be 3 feet tall, while for jackets of different types it is advisable for the space to be 4 feet tall. It is also recommendable to keep a distance of 0.8 inches between one item of clothing and another to protect the cloth.

PARA ROPA LARGA Y PANTALONES que se cuelgo con su largo es necesario contar con módulos de 1.50 de alto; para camisas y pantalones doblados los tub de colgado deben alcanzar los 90 cm de altura, para sacos y chamarras conviene que tengan un al de 1.20 m. Se recomienda dejar 2 cm entre prenda prenda para que las telas no se maltraten.

JUR LES VETEMENTS LONGS ET LES PANTALONS
pendus en longueur, prévoir des modules de 1.50 m
hauteur ; pour les chemises et les pantalons pliés,
tube de la penderie doit être placé à 90 cm de
uteur et à 1.20 m de hauteur pour les vestes et les
ousons. Il est conseillé de ménager un écart de 2 cm
tre chaque cintre afin d'éviter les frottements entre
vêtements.

FÜR KLEIDUNG UND HOSEN, die lang aufgehängt
werden, benötigt man Module mit einer Höhe von
1.50 m; für Hemden und gefaltete Hosen müssen die
Stangen sich auf einer Höhe von 0.90 m befinden
und für Sakkos und Jacken ist eine Höhe von 1.20 m
angebracht. Es ist empfehlenswert 2 cm Platz zwischen
den Kleidungsstücken zu lassen, damit die Stoffe nicht
in Mitleidenschaft gezogen werden.

A cube in the middle of the dressing room allows you to make maximum use of space. For instance, we could put drawers all along its perimeter and take advantage of its depth. If the rest of the storage furniture is fixed along the perimeter and set against the wall, usage of space will be optimized.

Un cubo al centro del vestidor permitirá aprovechar el espacio de manera generosa, pues se podrá colocar a todo su perímetro cajones beneficiándose de su profundidad. Si además el resto del mobiliario de guardado se proyecta perimetralmente y adosado a muros, el rendimiento espacial será inmejorable.

Pour tirer un parti maximal de l'espace disponible, placer un cube au centre du dressing et placer des caissons tout le long des murs. Si le dressing est aménagé de façon à ce que tous les modules de rangement soient adossés aux murs, vous obtiendrez un rendement optimum de votre espace.

Ein Möbel in der Mitte des Ankleidezimmers erlaubt eine grosszügige Nutzung des vorhandenen Raumes. Hier können Schubladen eingeplant werden, die es erlauben auf die gesamte Tiefe zuzugreifen. Wenn dann noch die restlichen Möbel aussen herum an den Wänden angeordnet werden, ist die Nutzung des Platzes optimal.

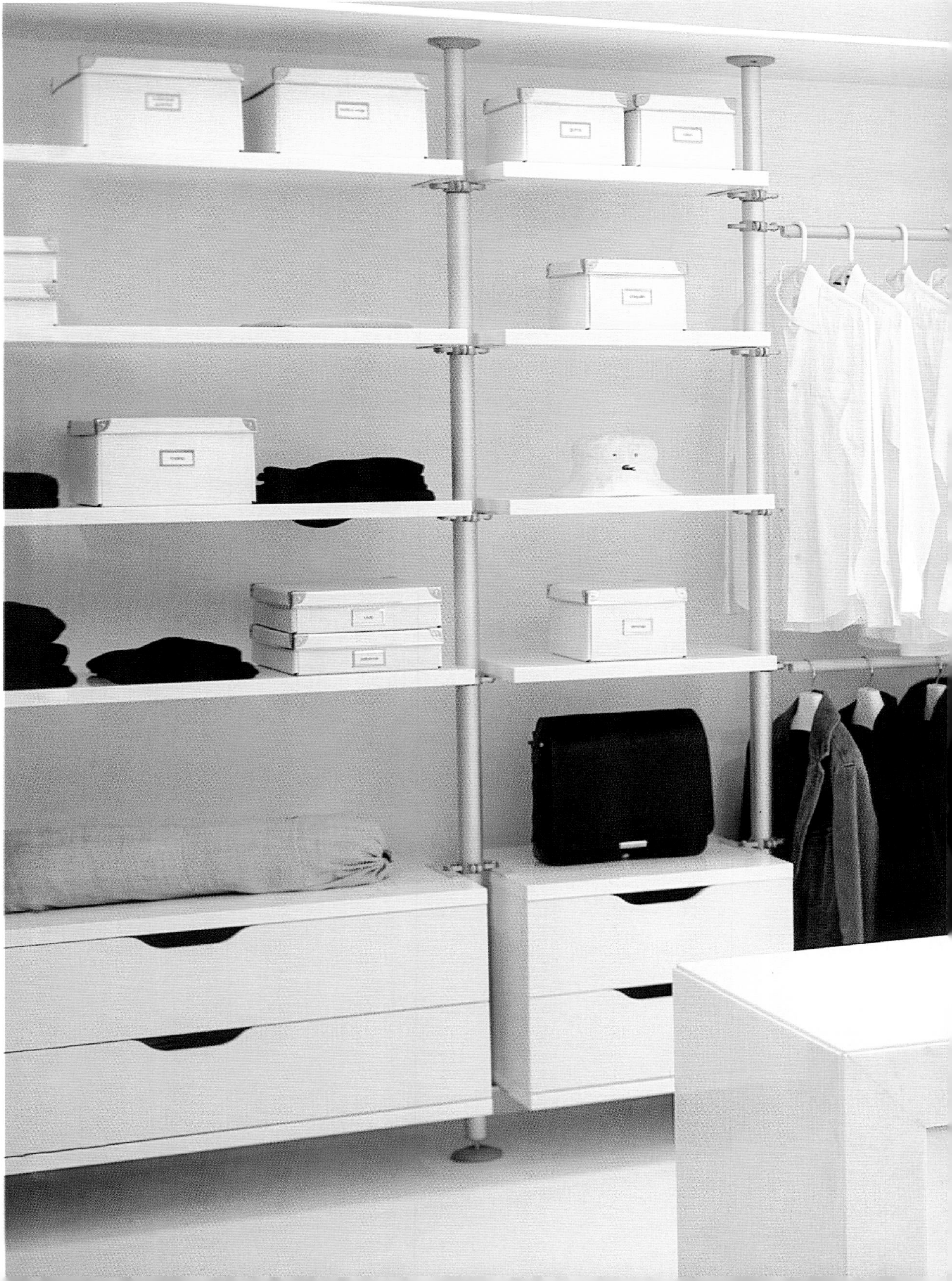

Storage systems with internal divisions and drawers are recommended for dressing rooms, as they offer specialization and allow the wardrobe to be arranged in accordance with the frequency of use of the clothing. Storage space must be clearly defined with the possibility of unambiguous classification. Elements such as glass doors are ideal for closing off certain areas that allow clothing to be viewed and, at the same time, protect it from dust. A smooth, easy-to-clean cover is also ideal for placing items of clothing on when they are selected.

Para los vestidores se recomiendan los sistemas de almacenaje con divisiones interiores y cajoneras, pues ofrecen especialidad y facilitan la organización del guardarropa de acuerdo, incluso, con la frecuencia de uso de las prendas. El espacio de almacenamiento debe estar claramente dispuesto y con posibilidad de una buena clasificación. Son ideales algunos elementos como puertas de vidrio para cerrar determinadas áreas que al mismo tiempo que permiten que se distinga la vestimenta, la protegen del polvo. También resulta óptima la existencia de una cubierta lisa y de limpieza sencilla para colocar la ropa al momento de elegirla.

Il est recommandé d'équiper le dressing de modules munis de séparations internes et de caissons ; vous pourrez ainsi attribuer une spécialisation à chaque compartiment et organiser votre garde-robe par type de vêtements et par fréquence d'utilisation. L'espace de rangement doit être clairement disposé et faciliter le classement des vêtements. Les portes en verre permettent d'isoler certains compartiments et de protéger leur contenu ; en un coup d'œil, vous saurez quels sont les vêtements qui y sont rangés. Pour le meuble sur lequel vous posez les vêtements que vous allez mettre, choisir un revêtement lisse et facile à nettoyer.

Für Ankleidezimmer sind Systeme mit Innenaufteilungen und Schubladen angebracht, da sie die Organisation des Kleiderschrankes je nach Kleidungsstück oder sogar nach der Häufigkeit des Gebrauches ermöglichen. Der Platz zum Aufbewahrung von Kleidung sollte klar eingeteilt sein. Zum Verschliessen bestimmter Bereiche sind Elemente wie Glastüren ideal, da sie gleichzeitig den Blick auf den Inhalt ermöglichen und vor Staub schützen. Ebenfalls ideal ist eine glatte und leicht zu reinigende Ablage, die während der Auswahl der Kleidung hilfreich ist.

If you choose multiple drawers as your storage system, the visible side should preferably be made of transparent material, as this allows you to see what's inside without needing to open it. Another option is open furniture with shelves on which you can see the content.

Si se seleccionan cajoneras múltiples como sistema de guardado conviene que su cara visible sea de material transparente, ello ofrece la ventaja de ver lo que hay dentro sin necesidad de abrirlas. Otra opción son los muebles abiertos con repisas que dejan a la vista el contenido.

Si vous choisissez un système de rangement à tiroirs, il est préférable que la face externe soit transparente afin que vous sachiez ce que contient chaque tiroir sans avoir à l'ouvrir. Vous pouvez aussi préférer des meubles sans portes dont le contenu soit visible de l'extérieur.

Wenn mehrere Schubladen als Aufbewahrungssystem gewählt werden, ist es empfehlenswert die sichtbare Seite aus durchsichtigem Material zu fertigen, denn dies bietet den Vorteil, dass man ihren Inhalt sehen kann ohne sie öffnen zu müssen. Eine weitere Möglichkeit sind offene Möbel mit Regalbrettern und freiem Blick auf den Inhalt.

Drawers should have interior divisions, which should not be very tall; each section can be used to store something depending on its function and size.

Es ideal que los cajones cuenten con divisiones interiores y que no sean muy altos; cada apartado se puede destinar a guardar cosas de acuerdo con sus funciones y tamaños.

L'idéal est que les caissons ou modules ne soient pas placés trop haut et qu'ils soient munis de divisions internes ; vous pourrez ainsi ranger vos vêtements et accessoires conformément à leurs fonctions et à leurs dimensions.

Es ist ideal, wenn die Schubladen über eine Innenaufteilung verfügen und nicht sehr hoch sind. In jedem Fach können je nach Funktion und Grösse andere Dinge aufbewahrt werden.

Storage areas for clothing must be sufficiently fresh and kept away from the damp areas of the bathroom. They should also have sufficient drawers and containers that are appealing to the eye and allow this space to be arranged.

Los lugares de guardado de ropa deben ser muy frescos y estar separados de las zonas húmedas del baño; tener cajoneras y contenedores suficientes que, además de ser estéticos, cumplan con funciones prácticas y faciliten el orden en este espacio.

Les dressings et placards à vêtements doivent être frais et ne pas être placés trop près de la salle de bains en raison de l'humidité. Ils doivent être munis de caissons et de compartiments leur permettant de remplir une fonction esthétique en plus de leur fonction première.

Die Bereiche zum Aufbewahren von Kleidung müssen trocken sein und sich in bestimmter Entfernung von den Feuchtzonen des Badezimmers befinden. Ferner sollten sie genügend Schubladen und Fächer aufweisen, die nicht nur ästhetisch aussehen, sondern auch praktische Funktionen erfüllen und die Ordnung in diesem Bereich erleichtern.

IF THERE IS ONE PART OF THE HOME that needs furniture with lots of storage space but takes up little room, it is the bathroom. However, the dampness, heat and constantly changing temperatures can damage it if it is made of wood. It is recommendable to use weather-proof types of wood, such as Cuban tamarind or teak, and to cover the surface with synthetic sealants and waterproof paint, especially if it is located in the damp area. Another option is to use stone to cover areas that come into contact with water.

athroom furniture
nuebles de baño
meubles de bains
adezimmermöbel

SI EN ALGÚN ÁREA es necesario mobiliario con mucha capacidad y que ocupe poco espacio es en el baño; pero la humedad, el calor y los cambios de temperatura ocasionan el desgaste y deterioro cuando éste es de madera. Es recomendable utilizar tipos de madera resistentes a la intemperie, como el tzalam o la teka, y recubrir las superficies con selladores sintéticos y pinturas impermeabilizantes, sobre todo cuando se encuentran dentro del área húmeda. Otro recurso es utilizar cubiertas pétreas en las zonas de contacto con el agua.

SI UNE ZONE requiert d'un mobilier d'une grande capacité mais occupant peu d'espace, c'est bien la salle de bains. Rappelons toutefois que les meubles en bois résistent mal à l'humidité, à la chaleur et aux changements de température. Il est donc recommandé de choisir des bois résistants aux intempéries (teck ou tzalam-lysiloma bahamense) et d'isoler et d'imperméabiliser vos surfaces à l'aide de produits synthétiques et de peintures, surtout s'agissant des surfaces en contact avec l'humidité. Vous pouvez également choisir une surface pierreuse pour les zones en contact direct avec l'humidité.

WENN IN EINEM BEREICH Möbel mit viel Stauraum und wenig Platzbedarf benötigt werden, dann ist dies im Bad. Aber die Feuchtigkeit, die Hitze und die Temperaturschwankungen verursachen im Falle von Holzmöbeln Abnutzung und Verschleiss. Es ist daher empfehlenswert Holztypen zu verwenden, die diesen Bedingungen standhalten, so wie Tzalam oder Teakholz. Die Oberflächen sollten mit synthetischen Mitteln oder wasserabweisenden Farben versiegelt sein, vor allem wenn sie sich im direkten Feuchtbereich befinden. Eine andere Möglichkeit ist die Verwendung von steinartigen Oberflächen in den Bereiches mit Wasserkontakt.

CABINETS MADE FROM LIGHT COLORED WOOD such as oak, maple or birch afford a tasteful look and, when combined with mirrors or translucent or opaque glass, take on a more sophisticated appearance. The height of the walls can be put to great use by making storage spaces behind the mirrors, and their reflections will be ideal. The shelves in these areas should be installed at different heights and spaced sufficiently for placing easy-to-find items on them.

LOS GABINETES DE MADERAS CLARAS como el roble, el arce o el abedul ofrecen una apariencia elegante, combinados con espejo y cristal translúcido u opaco adquieren un aspecto sofisticado. Aprovechar la altura de los muros para generar espacio de guardado a espaldas de los espejos es de gran utilidad, además de que sus reflejos serán ideales. Conviene que las repisas dentro de estas áreas sean instaladas a distintas alturas y con un escalonamiento suficiente para colocar objetos de diversas dimensiones que resulten de fácil ubicación.

LE BOIS CLAIR (chêne, érable, bouleau) donne de l'élégance aux placards qui peuvent prendre un aspect sophistiqué grâce à l'ajout d'un miroir ou d'une vitre translucide ou opaque. Pensez à utiliser la hauteur des murs pour créer des espaces de rangement derrière de grands miroirs qui apporteront une sensation d'espace. De préférence, placez les étagères à des hauteurs différentes afin de pouvoir y ranger facilement des objets de dimensions diverses.

MÖBEL AUS HELLEN HOLZARTEN wie Eiche, Ahorn oder Birke sorgen für einen eleganten Anblick und kombiniert mit Spiegeln und durchsichtigem oder mattem Glas, wird ein moderner Eindruck erzielt. Ein Ausnutzen der Mauerhöhe zum Schaffen von Stauraum auf der Rückseite der Spiegel ist von grossem Nutzen. Ausserdem sind so die Lichtreflexe ideal. Es ist angebracht, dass die Regalbretter in diesem Bereich auf verschiedenen Höhen und in Stufenform angebracht werden, damit Objekte unterschiedlicher Grösse untergebracht und leicht aufgefunden werden können.

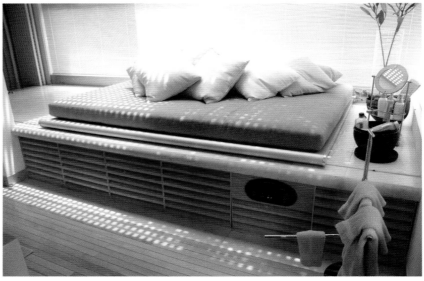

Wooden boudoirs topped by stone are not only protected from dampness but also create a contrast between materials that could have a great decorative impact. This effect can be enhanced by using stone with whitish tones alongside very dark wood, as well as by the shine and reflections from mirrors, metal handles and faucets. The greenery of plants, the toughness of baskets weaved from vegetable fibers and the delicacy of textiles and porcelain all conspire to create a touch of sheer fantasy.

Los tocadores de madera con cubiertas pétreas no sólo protegen al mueble de la humedad, sino también generan un contraste entre materiales que puede resultar de alto impacto decorativo. Es posible acrecentar este efecto usando la piedra en tonos blanquecinos junto a maderas muy oscuras, así como aprovechando los brillos y reflejos concebidos por los espejos, las jaladeras de metal y la grifería. El verdor de las plantas, la fuerza de los cestos tejidos con fibras vegetales y la delicadeza de los textiles y porcelanizados cooperan a dar el toque fantástico.

les tables de toilette en bois, placez une plaque en matériau pierreux qui protègera votre meuble de l'humidité et créera
contraste saisissant et agréable à l'œil. Vous pouvez améliorer cet effet en choisissant un dessus en pierre claire posé sur un
pport en bois très foncé, en jouant sur le reflet des miroirs, le contraste avec l'éclat des poignées métalliques et la robinetterie.
ur parachever le tout, ajoutez des plantes vertes, des paniers en fibre végétale, des tissus et des objets en porcelaine.

schtische mit steinartigen Oberflächen schützen nicht nur das Möbel vor Feuchtigkeit, sondern bieten auch einen
ntrast zwischen den Materialien, der höchst dekorativ sein kann. Dieser Effekt wird noch vergrössert, wenn Steine mit
sslichen Farbtönen mit sehr dunklen Holztönen sowie dem Glanz und Lichtreflexen der Spiegel, Metallgriffe und Armaturen
nbiniert werden. Das Grün der Pflanzen, aus Planzenfasern gewebten Körbe, zarte Stoffen und Porzellan sorgen für einen
tastischen Touch.

Bathroom furniture drawers can be used for keeping boudoir items; some may have pull-out racks that, in addition to being functional, allow certain objects to breathe and dry. An auxiliary element for drawers is rails that can be used to make additional compartments and divisions.

Los cajones en los muebles de baño sirven para guardar los artículos de tocador; algunos pueden contar con rejillas extraíbles que, aparte de ser funcionales, dejan que determinados objetos respiren y se sequen. Un método auxiliar para los cajones son las barandillas para crear compartimientos y divisiones adicionales.

Les tiroirs des meubles de salle de bains vous permettent de ranger vos affaires de toilettes. Certains meubles peuvent être équipés de paniers métalliques coulissants très fonctionnels et aérés dans lesquels vos affaires de toilette pourront sécher. Vous pouvez également créer des divisions et des compartiments supplémentaires dans vos tiroirs à l'aide de séparateurs.

Die Schubladen in den Badezimmermöbeln werden dazu verwendet, Toilettenartikel aufzubewahren. Einige können ausziehbare Gitter aufweisen, die sehr zweckmässig sind und auch dafür sorgen, dass bestimmte Objekte atmen und trocknen. Um in den Schubladen Ordnung zu halten, können Abtrennungen angebracht werden, um zusätzliche Fächer und Einteilungen zu schaffen.

An interesting option for cabinet doors in warm, tropical climates is the use of materials such as bamboo, rattan, sticks and wicker. These items lend furniture a rustic and artistic air. Bamboo can be made to shine by rubbing lemon juice all over its surface.

Una alternativa interesante para usar en las puertas de gabinetes en climas tropicales y calurosos la conformar materiales como el bambú, el rattan, la varilla y el mimbre; éstos otorgan al mueble una apariencia rústica y artesanal. El brillo del bambú se consigue si de vez en cuando se le pasa medio limón por toda la superficie.

zone tropicale ou sous les climats chauds, il est
intéressant d'utiliser des matériaux tels que le bambou,
rotin, l'osier ou les tiges de bambou qui donnent aux
meubles un aspect rustique et artisanal. Pour faire briller un
meuble en bambou, il suffit de le frotter de temps à autres
avec un demi citron.

Eine interessante Alternative für die Schranktüren bei
warmem oder tropischem Klima stellen Materialien wie
Bambus, Rattan und Korbgeflecht dar. Sie verleihen dem
Möbel ein rustikales Aussehen. Der Glanz des Bambus
bleibt erhalten, wenn die gesamte Oberfläche ab und an
mit einer halben Zitrone abgerieben wird.

Baskets weaved from hard and semi-hard vegetable fibers are economical and make ideal storage furniture in bathrooms; they also look better when lined with canvas or some other type of tough material on the inside.

Los canastos tejidos hechos de fibras vegetales duras y semiduras son económicos y pueden perfectamente funcionar como muebles de guardado en baños; su vista es más agradable cuando en el interior son revestidos con forros de lona o cualquier otro tipo de tela resistente.

Les paniers et corbeilles en fibre végétale dure ou mi-dure sont des objets bon marché qui peuvent parfaitement faire office de meuble de rangement dans une salle de bains. Ils sont plus agréables à regarder s'ils sont garnis de toile de chanvre ou de tout autre tissu résistant.

Harte und weiche Körbe aus Pflanzenfasern sind preisgünstig und können sehr gut als Stauraum zum Aufbewahren von Dingen im Badezimmer verwendet werden. Ihr Anblick ist schöner, wenn sie innen mit Plastik oder einem anderen widerstandsfähigen Stoff ausgekleidet sind.

A floating cabinet is easy to clean at the bottom where it joins the wall, which stops the wood from getting damp. A washbasin can be placed on top of it or to one side of it on top of another item of furniture. If the surface of the furniture is well varnished and the natural color of the wood can be appreciated, it will look appealing. White furniture tends to have a more hygienic feel. It can be closed at the push of a button or by using handles; but in either case, the closing device shou operate perfectly.

Los gabinetes volados facilitan la limpieza de la parte inferior en donde se empotran y evitan que la madera se humedezc Sobre ellos se puede colocar el lavabo o bien en un costado en un mueble adicional. Cuando las superficies de los muebles están bien barnizadas y exhiben la madera en su color natural dan buena apariencia, aunque un aspecto muy higiénico se consigue con mobiliario en color blanco. Las opciones de cerrado pueden ser a presión o a través de jaladeras, en cualquier caso, su funcionamiento debe ser óptimo.

fond des meubles suspendus au mur est facile à nettoyer ; n'étant pas en contact avec le sol, le bois est à l'abri de
umidité. Le lavabo peut-être installé dessus ou sur un autre élément disposé à côté. Afin d'obtenir un bel effet, bien vernir
surfaces et laisser transparaître la couleur et la moirure du bois naturel. Pour un aspect plus hygiénique, choisir des
eubles blancs. Pour la fermeture des portes, on a le choix entre les poignées ou la fermeture à pression. Qu'elle que soit la
ution, la fermeture doit être parfaite

ngende Schränke, die an den Wänden befestigt werden, erleichtern die Reinigung der unteren Bereiche. So wird vermieden,
ss das Holz Feuchtigkeit aufnimmt. Auf ihnen oder daneben in einem zusätzlichen Möbel, kann das Waschbecken
gebracht werden. Wenn die Oberflächen der Möbel versiegelt sind und der natürliche Holzton durchscheint, ist dies
r ästhetisch. Obwohl es hygienischer aussieht, wenn weisse Möbel verwendet werden. Als Schliesssystem können ein
agnetsystem oder Griffe verwendet werden. Wichtig ist dabei, dass das gewählte System optimal funktioniert.

auxiliary areas
zonas auxiliares
espaces secondaires
sonstige bereiche

THE WORD CELLAR refers to basements and, by extension, to the areas in which wine is stored. Private bars and cellars house collections closely linked to personal passions and preferences; factors such as dampness, light, temperature, conditions for maturing, ventilation, and thermal and acoustic isolation must be taken into consideration in their design, along with the presence of smells and contamination by parasites. Both the spaces themselves and the furniture must face north.

LA PALABRA CAVA significa bodega; se refiere a los sótanos en los que se produce el vino y se aplica por extensión a los espacios en donde éste se guarda. Las cavas y bares privados albergan colecciones relacionadas con aficiones y apegos personales; en su diseño deben considerarse factores de humedad, luz, temperatura, reposo, ventilación y aislamientos térmico

cústico, así como los concernientes al recogimiento de olores y a la
ntaminación de parásitos. Tanto los espacios como sus muebles deben
orientados al norte.

MOT CAVE fait référence aux caves à vins souterraines des viticulteurs ; par
ension, il s'applique aux espaces intérieurs où l'on conserve les bouteilles
vin. Les caves et les bars servent à abriter et à classer les collections des
ateurs selon leurs goûts personnels. Au niveau de leur conception, il faut
ir compte de l'humidité, de la lumière, de la température, de l'aération,
l'isolation thermique et acoustique, de la protection contre les vibrations,
odeurs et les parasites. L'espace aussi bien que le mobilier doivent être
entés au nord.

S WORT WEINKELLER bezieht sich ursprünglich auf den Keller, in dem
Wein hergestellt wird und wird heute auch für den Ort angewandt, an
m der Wein aufbewahrt wird. Weinkeller und private Bars bieten Raum
n Aufbewahren von Sammlungen je nach persönlichen Vorlieben und
gungen. In Bezug auf das Design müssen Faktoren wie die Feuchtigkeit,
nperatur, Ruhe, Lüftung und thermische sowie akustische Isolation in
racht gezogen werden. Auch die Beseitigung von Gerüchen und
unreinigung durch Parasiten muss berücksichtigt werden. Sowohl die
ume als auch die Möbel sollten in Richtung Norden ausgerichtet sein.

cellars and bars
cavas y bares
caves et bars
weinkeller und bars

FURNITURE WITH MODULAR RACKS are an excellent option for storing bottles, because they don't take up much space and can hold large volumes. The best woods for building them include oak and poplar, which are tough, virtually odorless and do not contaminate the wine, which tends to absorb the odor of the materials surrounding it over time. Some racks should be straight and others curved in order to contain bottles of different shapes and sizes.

LOS MUEBLES CON REJILLAS MODULARES son una excelente opción para almacenar botellas, pues ocupan poco espacio y permiten el acopio de grandes cantidades. Entre las maderas más adecuadas para construirlos se encuentran el encino y el álamo pues, además de ser resistentes, son prácticamente inodoras y no contaminan al vino, el cual con el tiempo tiende a absorber el olor de los materiales que lo circundan. Es preferible que algunos módulos tengan perfil de formas rectas y otros perfiles curvos, ello para dar soporte a diversos tamaños y tipos de botellas.

LES MEUBLES MUNIS DE PANIERS METALLIQUES MODULAIRES conviennent parfaitement au stockage des bouteilles : ils ont une grande capacité mais n'occupent que peu de place. Ces meubles doivent être de préférence en peuplier ou en chêne qui sont des bois à la fois résistants et pratiquement inodores, ce qui est important car le vin a tendance au fil des années à absorber l'odeur des matériaux qui se trouvent à proximité. Il est conseillé de mêler modules rectilignes et modules courbes afin de pouvoir ranger tous les types et tailles de bouteilles.

MÖBEL MIT MODULAREN EINTEILUNGEN stellen eine hervorragende Alternative zum Aufbewahren von Flaschen dar, da sie wenig Platz in Anspruch nehmen und die Unterbringung von grossen Mengen möglich machen. Zum den Hölzern, die sich am besten für solche Möbel eignen, zählen Eiche und Pappel, denn sie sind nicht nur widerstandsfähig, sondern nehmen auch praktisch keine Gerüche auf und verunreinigen so den Wein nicht, der mit der Zeit dazu tendiert, die Gerüche der umgebenden Materialien aufzunehmen. Es ist angebracht, dass einige Module gerade und andere gewölbte Formen aufweisen, so können verschiedene Grössen und Arten von Flaschen untergebracht werden.

Cellar and bar furniture may be designed in accordance with specific needs and the space available. There are a numbe of adaptable prefabricated options, such as trays, glass holders, racks, drawers with compartments, as well as others. Anoth option is to incorporate a temperature regulating device into the furniture to help maintain constant temperature, along wit anti-vibration mechanisms and apparatuses that absorb excessive dampness and then expel it during dry periods, thereby creating a microclimate in the cellar.

En la actualidad, el diseño del mobiliario para bar y cava puede ser planeado según las necesidades específicas de cada uno y a la medida del espacio, pues existe un buen número de elementos prefabricados con técnicas de ajuste como bandejas, portacopas, rejillas, cajoneras con divisiones, entre otros. También hay la posibilidad de incorporar al mueble sistemas de climatización que ayudan a conservar tanto la temperatura como la humedad a niveles constants que además están dotados de métodos antivibraciones. Estos aparatos permiten tener el ambiente adhoc para los vin creando un microclima en la cava.

À l'heure actuelle, le design du mobilier pour les bars et les caves peut être choisi en fonction des besoins spécifiques de chacun et de l'espace disponible ; il existe en effet un grand nombre d'éléments préfabriqués adaptables - plateaux, paniers métalliques, caissons à compartiments, etc.. Ces meubles peuvent être équipés d'un système de climatisation permettant de conserver les vins à température constante et de dispositifs absorbant les vibrations et l'humidité excessive pour l'expulser en période de sécheresse, créant ainsi un microclimat interne.

Heute kann das Design für Bars und Weinkeller genau nach den spezifischen Bedürfnissen und dem jeweiligen Platzangebot geplant werden. Es stehen viele vorgefertigte Elemente zur Verfügung, die durch Ablagen, Gläserhalter, Gitter, Schubladen mit Innenaufteilung usw. an die jeweiligen Erfordernisse angepasst werden können. Ausserdem können in die Möbel Klimaanlagen eingebaut werden, die dabei helfen die Temperatur gleichmässig zu halten. Ferner können auch Systeme zum Vermeiden von Vibrationen oder Apparate eingeplant werden, die die überschüssige Feuchtigkeit aufnehmen oder bei Trockenheit die Luft befeuchten, so dass ein Mikroklima im Inneren geschaffen wird.

Furniture for keeping bottles should preferably be set horizontally on walls that are permeable to the dampness of the earth, store up to 65 bottles per square meter and be surrounded by stone-like materials.

El mueble para apilar botellas debe de preferencia estar dispuesto horizontalmente sobre muros permeables a la humedad de la tierra, almacenar un máximo de 65 botellas por metro cuadrado y estar rodeado de materiales pétreos.

Le meuble contenant les bouteilles doit être placé dans un environnement en pierre, contre un mur perméable à l'humidité de la terre de façon à ce que les bouteilles soient couchées horizontalement. La capacité de rangement doit être de 65 bouteilles par m2 maximum.

Das Möbel zum Unterbringen von Flaschen sollte nach Möglichkeit waagerecht aufgeteilt sein und sich auf einer Mauer befinden, die die Feuchtigkeit der Erde durchlässt. Es sollten nicht mehr als 65 Flaschen auf einem Quadratmeter untergebracht werden und aussen herum sollten sich steinartige Materialien befinden.

For wine distribution purposes, the shelves should be deep enough so that bottles can be placed horizontally and the corks kept moistened. It is necessary to have differentiators to arrange the cellar in accordance with the grape, vintage and region of the wine.

Para la distribución de los vinos se sugiere que los estantes tengan la profundidad suficiente para que éstos sean colocados en forma horizontal y su corcho se mantenga humedecido. Es importante contar con espacios diferenciados para organizar la cava de acuerdo con los cepajes, cosechas y regiones.

Il est préférable que les étagères soient suffisamment profondes pour que les bouteilles soient couchées et que le bouchon soit toujours humide. Il est important de différencier les espaces de stockage afin de pouvoir organiser sa cave selon les crus, les appellations ou les cépages.

Zur Aufteilung der Weine ist es angebracht, dass die Regalbretter die ausreichende Tiefe aufweisen, um die Flaschen waagerecht lagern zu können, damit der Korken feucht bleibt. Es ist wichtig, dass der Weinkeller über verschieden grossen Stauraum verfügt, damit der Wein gemäss der Qualität, Ernten und Regionen aufgewahrt werden kann.

Cellar furniture must comply with wine storage standards. These include keeping the wine away from any sources of heat, strong smells and vibrations; the wood should not be aromatic nor exposed to natural or artificial light; constant temperature of between 10° and 16° C should be maintained, along with humidity levels of between 70 and 80 %.

El mobiliario de bodegas subterráneas debe cumplir con normas para el almacenamiento del vino tales como estar lejos de fuentes de calor, olores fuertes y vibraciones; no ser de madera aromática ni estar expuesto a la luz natural o artificial; permitir conservar una temperatura constante entre 10° y 16° C y una humedad entre 70 y 80 %.

mobilier des caves en sous-sol doit respecter les normes
blies pour la conservation du vin : être à l'abri des sources
chaleur, des odeurs et des vibrations, ne pas être en bois
matique ni être exposé à la lumière naturelle ou artificielle.
doit pouvoir y assurer une température constante comprise
re 10° C et 16° C et une humidité constante de 70% à 80%.

Möbel für unterirdische Lagerräume müssen Normen zur
inlagerung erfüllen, so wie zum Beispiel eine bestimmte
fernung von Wärmequellen, starken Gerüchen und
rationen. Sie dürfen ferner nicht aus aromatischen
zern bestehen und nicht künstlichem oder natürlichem
ht ausgesetzt sein. Es muss ferner möglich sein, ständig
e Temperatur zwischen 10° und 16° C aufrecht zu
alten sowie eine Feuchtigkeit zwischen 70 und 80 %.

A closet is a good option for storing liqueurs, wines and glassware, if you have enough modules, shelves, drawers and racks. It is advisable to have a mixing table and a bar close at hand, and for bench seats to be 13.5 inches below them.

Un armario puede ser buena opción para resguardar licores, vinos y cristalería si cuenta con suficientes módulos, estantes, cajoneras y rejillas. Se recomienda que tenga cerca una mesa para preparación y una barra, y que los asientos de los bancos queden a 30 cm de altura respecto a esta última.

L'armoire est un meuble pratique pour ranger les alcools, les vins et les verres à condition de l'avoir divisée en compartiments, caissons et supports. Placer à proximité de l'armoire une table qui vous servira à préparer les boissons. Pour le bar, prévoir un comptoir et des tabourets mesurant 30 cm de moins que le comptoir.

Ein Schrank kann keine gute Alternative zum Aufbewahren von Likör, Wein und Gläsern darstellen, wenn er mit ausreichenden Modulen, Regalbrettern, Schubladen und Gittern ausgestattet ist. Es ist empfehlenswert, einen Tisch oder eine Bar in der Nähe zu haben, auf dem die Getränke zubereitet werden können. Die entsprechenden Stühle sollten 30 cm niedriger als die Bar sein.

The surface of the bar must be made from easy-to-clean materials, such as marble, glass or wood. Its height and interior can be put to good use by fitting it with shelves and drawers.

Conviene que la superficie de la barra de bar sea de materiales de fácil limpieza como mármol, vidrio o madera; y que se aproveche su altura e interior equipando al mueble con repisas y cajones.

Pour la surface du comptoir, choisir de préférence un matériau facile à nettoyer comme le marbre, le verre ou le bois. Exploiter la hauteur du meuble pour y aménager des étagères, des caissons et des tiroirs.

Es ist angebracht, dass die Oberfläche der Bar aus einem Material besteht, das leicht zu reinigen ist, wie z.B. Mamor, Glas oder Holz. Ferner sollte die Höhe und das Innere ausgenutzt werden und das Möbel mit Regalbrettern und Schubladen ausgestattet sein.

Some items of furniture with air conditioning have glass doors with UV filters to stop ultraviolet rays from entering, and are fitted with sliding trays that allow wine to be classified in accordance with the grape.

Algunos muebles climatizados tienen puertas de vidrio con filtros UV para evitar la penetración de los rayos ultravioleta y están provistos de bandejas deslizantes que permiten clasificar a los vinos por cepas.

Certains meubles climatisés sont équipés de portes en verre teinté anti-UV qui évitent la pénétration des rayons ultraviolets. Ils sont parfois munis de plateaux coulissants permettant de classer les vins par appellation ou cépage.

Einige Möbel mit Klimaanlage haben Glastüren mit UV-Schutz, um ultraviolette Strahlen abzuhalten. Andere weisen Schubfächer auf, die es möglich machen den Wein je nach Qualität zu unterteilen.

CONSOLE TABLES AND CHESTS OF DRAWERS can be
decorative, perform a functional role or do both at once.
They are usually placed next to the entrance to houses
and against the wall. If they are located in the reception
or hall they can be used for keeping keys, money and
other articles to be taken into and out of the house, but
they can also make a contribution as ornaments. Chests
of drawers with a folding top or drawers look esthetically
pleasing and are ideal for keeping papers and files in.

LAS CONSOLAS Y CÓMODAS pueden satisfacer una necesidad decorativa, servir como objetos funcionales o ambas cosas. Generalmente son mesas hechas para colocarse en la entrada de las casas y junto a la pared. Cuando se les ubica en la recepción o vestíbulo pueden aprovecharse para guardar llaves, dinero y otros artículos que se requieren al entrar y salir de casa, pero también es posible destinarlas para colocar sobre ellas adornos. Aquéllas de tapa abatible o con cajones tienen una apariencia estéticamente agradable y funcionan también para guardar papeles y archivos.

LES CONSOLES ET LES COMMODES peuvent satisfaire des besoins décoratifs et/ou être utilisés comme objets utilitaires. Il s'agit généralement de meubles conçus pour être placés contre un mur dans le hall d'entrée. Quand ils se trouvent placés dans le vestibule ou dans l'entrée, on peut y ranger les clefs, l'argent liquide et les autres objets qu'on emporte avec soi quand on sort et dont on se débarrasse en rentrant; on peut aussi y poser des objets décoratifs. Les consoles à couvercle rabattable sont esthétiques et pratiques et permettent de ranger papiers, factures et dossiers.

consoles
consolas
consoles
konsolen

KONSOLEN UND KOMMODEN können einen dekorativen Zweck erfüllen, als funktionelles Möbel verwendet werden oder beides gleichzeitig. Im Allgemeinen handelt es sich um Tische, die im Eingangsbereich an die Wand gestellt werden. Wenn sie im Empfangsbereich oder Hausflur aufgestellt werden, können sie zum Aufbewahren von Schlüsseln, Geld oder anderen Artikeln verwendet werden, die bei Betreten und Verlassen des Hauses benötigt werden. Sie können aber auch als Basis für dekorative Elemente dienen. Konsolen mit einer aufklappbaren Abdeckung oder Schubladen sind ästhetisch und gleichzeitig kann man dort auch Papiere unterbringen.

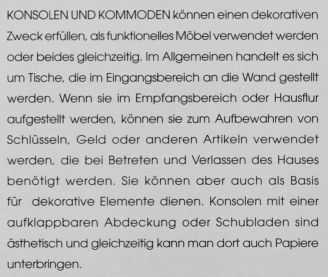

The filing cabinet is a popular item of furniture that comes in various styles and materials. It is wider than a console table; it often has doors and drawers or just drawers. It is frequently used in entrance halls and commonly accompanied by a large object, such as a mirror, a painting or a vase that help balance the space. As far as storage is concerned, it is considered an auxiliary piece of furniture, with little capacity, but useful for keeping directories, agendas, keys, correspondence and documents for immediate use, such as gas or electricity bills.

El taquillón es un mueble popular, posible de encontrar en diversos estilos y materiales. Su anchura es mayor que la de la consola; regularmente tiene puertas y cajones o sólo cajones. Se usa en el recibidor y es común que se le acompañe de un objeto de buena dimensión como un espejo, un cuadro o un florero que cooperen a equilibrar el espacio. En términos de guardado se le considera un mueble auxiliar, de poca capacidad, útil para directorios, agendas, llaves, corresponden y papeles de uso inmediato como cuentas de gas o luz.

buffet bas est un meuble populaire qu'on trouve sous différentes formes et en différents matériaux. Il est plus profond u'une console et est généralement muni de tiroirs et de compartiments fermés ou uniquement de tiroirs. On trouve ce enre de meubles dans les halls, surmonté, pour mieux équilibrer l'espace, d'un objet de grande taille (miroir, tableau ou and vase). Il s'agit de meubles d'appoint d'une capacité de rangement plutôt faible, où l'on rangera les annuaires, les ertoires, les clefs, le courrier et les factures urgentes.

ne Garderobe ist ein beliebtes Möbelstück, das in verschiedenen Stilrichtungen und aus verschiedenen Materialien efertigt sein kann. Dieses Möbel ist breiter als eine Konsole und für gewöhnlich weist es Türen und Schubladen oder nur hubladen auf. Es wird im Eingangsbereich verwendet und normalerweise ist auch ein grosses Objekt enthalten, wie ein iegel, ein Gemälde oder eine Blumenvase, die dabei helfen, das Gleichgewicht des Raumes zu halten. In Bezug auf den auraum gilt es als Hilsfmöbel mit wenig Platz, das zum Verstauen von Verzeichnissen, Kalendern, Schlüsseln, Briefen oder pieren, wie z.B. Strom- und Gasrechnung verwendet wird.

Chests of drawers designed in terms of straight lines are ideal for creating horizontal and vertical angular combinations supported by the inclusion of additional volumes or surfaces that can sit on top of them, either partially or totally. This alternative affords mobility to the space, as well as boosting the functionality and esthetic quality of the furniture. Another option for making the furniture more dynamic and toning down its visual impact is to combine colors and finishes. For instance, one tone can be used on general surfaces and another on the drawers.

Las cómodas cuyo diseño se compone básicamente de líneas rectas admiten que se generen juegos horizontales y verticales a partir de la incorporación de volúmenes adicionales o de entrepaños que pueden encimarse ya sea de form parcial o total. Este recurso dota de movimiento al espacio extendiendo la funcionalidad y la estética del mobiliario. Una alternativa más para dar dinamismo al mueble y aligerar su peso visual es la combinación de colores y acabados; se puede utilizar un tono en las superficies generales y otro en los cajones.

commodes au design rectiligne permettent des jeux horizontaux et verticaux à partir de modules ou de panneaux
cés les uns au-dessus des autres. On donne ainsi une impression de mouvement à l'espace et on ajoute à la valeur
ctionnelle et esthétique du mobilier. Pour donner plus de dynamisme à votre commode et lui donner une allure moins
ssive, vous pouvez mêler les couleurs et les revêtements, en employant, par exemple, une couleur pour les contours du
uble et une autre pour les tiroirs.

nmoden, die fast ausschliesslich aus geraden Linien bestehen, können durch waagerechte oder senkrechte Details
gelockert werden, wie z.B. zusätzlicher Stauraum, Regalbretter, die über die gesamte Fläche gehen oder nur einzelne
eiche abdecken. So werden die glatten Flächen aufgelockert und das Möbel sieht ästhetischer aus. Eine andere
ernative zur Verringerung des visuellen Gewichtes sind Kombinationen verschiedener Farben und Oberflächen; es kann
Farbton für die gesamten Oberflächen und ein anderer für die Schubladen gewählt werden.

The solid look of a sideboard or chest of drawers can be enhanced if these items of furniture are deprived of any type of ornaments or strips, the natural color and grain of the wood are displayed, and the standard handles are replaced by more subtle closing mechanisms, such as pressure-based ones.

Es factible acentuar el aspecto de solidez de un aparador o cómoda puede acentuarse si se exceptúan de éstos todo tipo de ornamentos y molduras, se muestra el color natural y el veteado de su madera, y se sustituyen las clásicas jaladeras por métodos de cerrado ocultos o a presión.

L'aspect massif d'un buffet bas ou d'une commode peut être accentué en les privant de tout ornement ou moulure; cet effet sera d'autant plus frappant si vous conservez la couleur et la moirure du bois naturel et que vous remplacez les poignées par des fermetures invisibles ou à pression.

Der massive Eindruck einer Anrichte oder Kommode kann vermindert werden, indem Verzierungen und Leisten angebracht werden, der natürliche Holzton und die Holzmaserung zu sehen sind und die klassischen Griffe durch verdeckte Schliess- oder Magnetsysteme ersetzt werden.

Dual purpose elements, that can serve as bookshelves on the visible side and hide the supports of the sofa on the non-visible side, are ideal for conjuring storage space out of nothing.

Los elementos de doble uso, que funcionan como estantería o librero por el lado visto y por el ciego sirven para ocultar los respaldos de los sofás, son ideales para generar espacio de guardado inexistente.

Les éléments faisant double usage, servant de face d'étagère ou de bibliothèque et de dos à dissimuler le dossier du canapé sont parfaits pour créer un espace de rangement là où il n'y en a pas.

Elemente mit Doppelfuntkion, wie Regale auf der Sichtseite, die auch dazu dienen, die Rückseiten von Sofas zu verdecken, sind ideal zum Schaffen von zusätzlichem Stauraum.

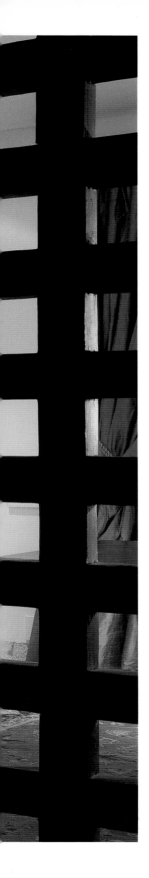

Extensively decorated furniture with relief ornaments may be excessive, especially nowadays when the trend favors furniture with a more subtle presence, but if they are strategically placed in a space where they can play a prominent role, they can provide a major esthetic contribution.

Los muebles de estilo profusamente decorados con tallas en relieve pueden resultar recargados sobre todo ahora que la tendencia se inclina por el mobiliario de poco peso visual, pero si se les coloca en un espacio donde se les otorgue un lugar protagónico pueden se convierten en claves.

Les meubles profusément décorés ou sculptés peuvent paraître surchargés surtout à notre époque où la tendance est aux lignes dépouillées. Toutefois, si vous les situez correctement dans l'espace, ils peuvent contribuer à donner une identité à la pièce.

Übermässig dekorierte Möbel mit reliefartigen Verzierungen können überladen wirken, vor allem, weil die Tendenz heute zu visuell leichten Möbeln geht. Werden sie allerdings an einen Ort gestellt, der nur diesem Möbelstück vorbehalten ist, so können sie gut zur Geltung kommen.

Console tables, trunks, chests and credence tables are storage furniture that were expelled from modern homes as from the mid-Twentieth Century, but they are now making a comeback as an option for complementing corners, corridors and entrance halls from both an esthetic and practical point of view. Obviously, given that some of them are not that easy to open, they can be used as a kind of decorative wine cellar, and inside of them objects can be placed that are never used but have been kept for their sentimental value.

Consolas, baúles, cofres y credenzas son muebles para guardar que desde mediados del siglo XX fueron desterrados de los hogares modernos y que vuelven a la actualidad constituyéndose en una alternativa para resolver esquinas, pasillos y vestíbulos desde el punto de vista estético y práctico. Desde luego, dado que algunos de ellos presentan dificultad o requieren de esfuerzo para abrirlos se les puede aprovechar como especie de bodegas decorativas y colocar dentro de ellos objetos que nunca se utilicen pero que se conservan porque tienen un valor estimativo.

consoles, bahuts, coffres et autres sont des meubles de rangement qui avaient déserté les foyers modernes aux alentours milieu du XX siècle. Ils reviennent à présent sous forme de meubles d'appoint destinés à équiper les coins des pièces, les uloirs et les vestibules tant du point de vue pratique que du point de vie esthétique. Étant donné que certains sont difficiles uvrir ou munis d'un couvercle trop lourd, on s'en sert de meubles décoratifs et on y range les objets dont on ne sert pas is auxquels on tient.

nsolen, Truhen und Kofferschränke sind Möbel zum Verstauen von Dingen, die seit Mitte des XX. Jahrhunderts aus den dernen Hauhalten verbannt wurden. Heute werden sie wieder dazu verwendet Ecken, Flure und den Eingangsbereich auf netische und praktische Weise als Stauram zu nutzen. Da einige dieser Stücke schwer zu öffnen sind, können sie als eine dekorativer Raum für Objekte genutzt werden, die so gut wie nie Verwendung finden, aber dennoch aufbewahrt werden, I sie einen bestimmten Wert haben.

Chiffoniers are slender pieces of furniture with many drawers. Once upon a time, they were used by women for keeping their jewels, letters, fabric and secrets in, but now they are in vogue and share the leading role with long and modern chests of drawers made from novel materials and pure lines.

Los chifoniers son cómodas estrechas con gavetas múltiples, que en otro momento se utilizaron para que las mujeres guardaran joyas, escritos, tejidos y sus secretos, hoy se ponen de moda y comparten el rol principal con largas y modernas cómodas fabricadas en materiales novedosos y líneas puras.

Les chiffonniers étaient des commodes étroites munies de nombreux tiroirs dans lesquels les femmes rangeaient jadis leurs bijoux, leur courrier, leur ouvrage et leurs petits secrets; ces meubles remis au goût du jour réapparaissent à présent sous forme de longues commodes aux lignes pures, fabriquées en matériaux contemporains.

Herrenkommoden sind dünne Kommoden mit mehreren Schubfächern, die einst von Frauen dazu verwandt wurden, ihren Schmuck, Briefe, Textilien und Geheimnisse aufzubewahren. Heute sind sie wieder modern und werden neben langen und modernen Kommoden verwendet, die aus neuartigen Materialien und mit klaren Linien gefertigt werden.

architectonic arquitectónicos architectoniques architektonisch

52 - 53 C'CÚBICA, emilio cabrero, andrea cesarman y marco a. coello buck

54 (top) MODA IN CASA, louis poiré

54 - 55 (bottom) MODA IN CASA, louis poiré

55 (top) C-CHIC, olga mussali h. y sara mizrahi e.

56 JBF ARQUITECTOS, josé luis barbará y josé fernández

57 C-CHIC, olga mussali h. y sara mizrahi e.

58 - 59 AGRAZ ARQUITECTOS, ricardo agraz

60 MARQCÓ, mariangel álvarez c. y covadonga hernández g.

61 (top) MARQCÓ, mariangel álvarez c. y covadonga hernández g., (bottom) DUPUIS, alejandra prieto de palacios y cecilia prieto de martínez g.

62 BH, BROISSIN Y HERNÁNDEZ DE LA GARZA, gerardo broissin y jorge hernández de la garza

64 - 65 MARQCÓ, mariangel álvarez c. y covadonga hernández g.

66 - 67 PAYEN ARQUITECTOS, jacques payen

68 juan carlos baumgartner

70 - 71 ezequiel farca

72 - 73 URBANA, alejandro escudero

74 (left) DUPUIS, alejandra prieto de palacios y cecilia prieto de martínez g.

74 - 75 ARMELLA ARQUITECTOS / DUPUIS, mario armella gullete y mario armella maza / alejandra prieto de palacios y cecilia prieto de martínez g.

75 (right) MEMORIA CASTIZA, marco polo hernández y leonor mastretta real

76 GRUPO LBC, alfonso lópez baz, javier calleja / alberto kalach y raúl pulido

77 A5 ARQUITECTURA, alejandro bernardi, gloria cortina, imanol legorreta, beatriz peschard y pablo sepúlveda

78 - 79 MEMORIA CASTIZA, marco polo hernández y leonor mastretta real

80 MIGDAL ARQUITECTOS, jaime varon, abraham metta y alex metta

81 ARMELLA ARQUITECTOS, mario armella gullete y mario armella maza

83 SAMA ARQUITECTOS, rafael sama

84 LARA + LARA ARQUITECTOS, víctor manuel lara m. y leonardo lara e.

85 ezequiel farca

86 - 87 ezequiel farca y mauricio gómez de tuddo

88 (bottom) COVILHA, avelino gonzález e., blanca gonzález de o., maribel gonzález de d. y mely gonzález de f.

88 - 89 (top) GUTIÉRREZ Y ALONSO ARQUITECTOS, ángel alonso chein y eduardo gutiérrez guzmán

89 (bottom) LA CASA DISEÑO DE INTERIORES, jennie g. de ruiz galindo y alejandro fernández d.

90 - 91 GA, GRUPO ARQUITECTURA, daniel álvarez

92 FM ESTUDIO DE ARQUITECTURA, esteban medrano u. y guillermo fernández r.

93 ADI, gina parlange pizarro

94 (top left) C-CHIC, olga mussali h. y sara mizrahi e., (top right and bottom) 7XA ARQUITECTURA, carlos ortíz y ángel lópez

95 (top) GRUPO LBC, alfonso lópez baz y javier calleja / gabriela senderos, raúl pulido, federico rivera rio y octavio cardozo, (bottom) LA CASA DISEÑO DE INTERIORES, jennie g. de ruiz galindo y alejandro fernández d.

96 - 97 GA, GRUPO ARQUITECTURA, daniel álvarez
98 alejandro bernardi gallo y beatriz peschard mijares
99 a 101 TERRÉS, javier valenzuela g., fernando
valenzuela g. y guillermo valenzuela g.
102 - 103 ADI / ABAX, gina parlange pizarro,
fernando de haro, jesús fernández, omar fuentes y
bertha figueroa
104 GRUPO LBC, alfonso lópez baz y javier calleja /
carlos majluf, raúl pulido y federico rivera rio
105 CC ARQUITECTOS S.A. DE C.V., manuel cervantes
céspedes y santiago céspedes morera
106 - 107 EL TERCER MURO, ARQUITECTURA E INTERIORISMO
S.A. DE C.V., enrique fuertes bojorges y jaime reyes
mendiola
108 ABAX / B+P, fernando de haro, jesús fernández,
omar fuentes y bertha figueroa / alejandro bernardi
gallo y beatriz peschard mijares
109 GRUPO LBC, alfonso lópez baz y javier calleja / raúl
pulido, federico rivera rio y simón hamui
110 BECKER ARQUITECTOS, moisés becker
111 ABAX, fernando de haro, jesús fernández, omar
fuentes y bertha figueroa
112 A5 ARQUITECTURA, alejandro bernardi, gloria cortina,
imanol legorreta, beatriz peschard y pablo sepúlveda
113 GRUPO AGM, patricio garcía muriel y fernando
abogado alonso
114 - 115 ABAX, fernando de haro, jesús fernández,
omar fuentes y bertha figueroa
116 COVILHA, blanca gonzález de o., maribel gonzález
de d. y claudia goudet de g.

117 DENTRO, javier sordo madaleno, ana paula de
haro y claudia lópez-duplán
118 - 119 DE YTURBE ARQUITECTOS, josé de yturbe bernal,
josé de yturbe sordo y andrés cajiga ramírez
120 - 121 GRUPO LBC / BECKER ARQUITECTOS, alfonso lópez
baz y javier calleja / moisés becker / raúl pulido
122 juan carlos baumgartner
123 SAMA ARQUITECTOS, rafael sama
124 BH, BROISSIN Y HERNÁNDEZ DE LA GARZA, gerardo
broissin y jorge hernández de la garza
125 GRUPO LBC, alfonso lópez baz y javier calleja /
carlos majluf, raúl pulido y federico rivera rio
126 CC ARQUITECTOS S.A. DE C.V., manuel cervantes
céspedes y santiago céspedes morera
127 EL TERCER MURO, ARQUITECTURA E INTERIORISMO S.A. DE
C.V., enrique fuertes bojorges y jaime reyes mendiola
128 - 129 C-CHIC, olga mussali h. y sara mizrahi e.
130 ABAX, fernando de haro, jesús fernández, omar
fuentes y bertha figueroa
131 (top) ARQUITECH, juan josé sánchez-aedo,
(bottom) ABAX, fernando de haro, jesús fernández,
omar fuentes y bertha figueroa
132 - 133 carlos lassala, elvira elenes y eduardo lassala
134 - 135 DE YTURBE ARQUITECTOS, josé de yturbe bernal,
josé de yturbe sordo y andrés cajiga ramírez
136 - 137 gerardo garcía l.
139 MARQCÓ, mariangel álvarez c. y covadonga
hernández g.
141 GRUPO LBC / CHK ARQUITECTOS, alfonso lópez baz y
javier calleja / eduardo hernández

142 C-CHIC, olga mussali h. y sara mizrahi e.

143 LA CASA DISEÑO DE INTERIORES, jennie g. de ruiz galindo y alejandro fernández d.

144 - 145 ADI / ABAX, gina parlange pizarro, fernando de haro, jesús fernández, omar fuentes y bertha figueroa

146 URBANA, alejandro escudero

147 (top and bottom) LA CASA DISEÑO DE INTERIORES, jennie g. de ruiz galindo y alejandro fernández d., (center) URBANA, alejandro escudero

148 - 149 MARQCÓ, mariangel álvarez c. y covadonga hernández g.

151 (top) ART ARQUITECTOS ASOCIADOS, antonio rueda ventosa, (bottom) GRUPO LBC / CHK, alfonso lópez baz y javier calleja / eduardo hernández

152 - 153 MEMORIA CASTIZA, marco polo hernández y leonor mastretta real

154 a 159 MARQCÓ, mariangel álvarez c. y covadonga hernández g.

160 a 163 GA, GRUPO ARQUITECTURA, daniel álvarez

164 - 165 ADI, gina parlange pizarro

166 GA, GRUPO ARQUITECTURA, daniel álvarez

167 ADI, gina parlange pizarro

168 - 169 BCO ARQUITECTOS, david gonzález blanco

170 - 171 gerardo garcía l.

172 DUPUIS, alejandra prieto de palacios y cecilia prieto de martínez g.

173 a 174 imanol legorreta y pablo sepúlveda

175 PASCAL ARQUITECTOS, carlos pascal wolf y gerard pascal wolf

177 (top) ARMELLA ARQUITECTOS, mario armella g. y mario armella m., (bottom) GUTIÉRREZ Y ALONSO ARQUITECTOS, ángel alonso chein y eduardo gutiérrez guzmán

178 ABAX, fernando de haro, jesús fernández, omar fuentes y bertha figueroa

179 CC ARQUITECTOS S.A. DE C.V., manuel cervantes céspedes y santiago céspedes morera

180 ADI / ABAX, gina parlange pizarro, fernando de haro, jesús fernández, omar fuentes y bertha figueroa

181 gerardo garcía l.

182 (top left) CC ARQUITECTOS S.A. DE C.V., manuel cervantes céspedes y santiago céspedes morera, (top right and bottom) ABAX, fernando de haro, jesús fernández, omar fuentes y bertha figueroa

185 BECKER ARQUITECTOS, moisés becker

186 TARME, alex carranza valles y gerardo ruiz díaz

187 RIVEROLL - RIVEROLL ARQUITECTOS, pablo riveroll otero y pedro riveroll otero

188 ABAX, fernando de haro, jesús fernández, omar fuentes y bertha figueroa

189 GRUPO ARQEE, pedro escobar f.v., jorge escalante p. y jorge carral d.

190 - 191 ARTECK, francisco guzmán giraud

192-193 ABAX, fernando de haro, jesús fernández, omar fuentes y bertha figueroa

194 - 195 (top) LA CASA DISEÑO DE INTERIORES, jennie g. de ruiz galindo y alejandro fernández d., (bottom) enrique zozaya

196 - 197 ABAX, fernando de haro, jesús fernández, omar fuentes y bertha figueroa

238 - 239 ezequiel farca

240 (left) DENTRO, javier sordo madaleno, ana paula
de haro y claudia lópez-duplán

240 - 241 gerardo garcía l.

242 - 243 MARQCÓ, mariangel álvarez c. y covadonga
hernández g.

244 - 245 alejandro bernardi gallo y beatriz peschard
mijares

246 (bottom) ezequiel farca y mauricio gómez de tuddo

246 - 247 (top) COVILHA, blanca gonzález de o.,
maribel gonzález de d. y claudia goudet de g.

247 (bottom) MARQCÓ, mariangel álvarez c. y
covadonga hernández g.

248 TERRÉS, javier valenzuela g., fernando valenzuela
g. y guillermo valenzuela g.

249 DE FIRMA, laura mercado patiño

250 (left) TERRÉS, javier valenzuela g., fernando
valenzuela g. y guillermo valenzuela g.

250 - 251 MARTÍNEZ-SORDO, juan salvador martínez y luis
martín sordo

252 - 253 ADI, gina parlange pizarro

254 (top left) ABAX, fernando de haro, jesús fernández,
omar fuentes y bertha figueroa, (top right and bottom
right) MARQCÓ, mariangel álvarez c. y covadonga
hernández g., (bottom left) TERRÉS, javier valenzuela g.,
fernando valenzuela g. y guillermo valenzuela g.

255 (top left) MARQCÓ, mariangel álvarez c. y
covadonga hernández g. (top right) GRUPO CORAGGIO,
rubén basurto gómez, (bottom) MARQCÓ, mariangel
álvarez c. y covadonga hernández g.

photographic   fotográficos   photographiques   fotografisch

alberto moreno - pgs. 81,.88-89 (top), 177 (top and bottom), 219 (top), 221 (top), 228 (bottom).

alejandro rodríguez - pgs. 27, 36.

alfonso de béjar - pgs. 51 (top), 93, 102-103, 144-145, 164-165, 167, 180, 237 (top), 252-253.

alfredo blasquez y alberto adame - pgs. 7 (center), 206-207.

andrés cortina - pgs. 89 (bottom), 95 (bottom), 143, 147 (top and bottom), 194 (top), 195 (top), 231 (bottom).

arturo zavala haag - pgs. 77, 112.

débora fossas - pg. 28 (bottom).

denisse escamilla - pgs. 40 (left), 41 (right), 151 (top), 227 (bottom).

estudio alectron - pgs. 22-23.

ezequiel farca - pg. 85.

federico de jesús - pgs. 11 (right), 18 a 20, 51 (bottom), 204-205.

fernando cordero - pgs. 110, 118-119, 185.

héctor armando herrera - pgs. 8, 230 (top).

héctor velasco facio - pgs. 7 (left and right), 10, 21, 30-31, 34-35, 38, 42-43, 46-47, 60 (top right and bottom), 61 (top), 64, 72-73, 88 (bottom), 95 (top), 98, 104, 108-109, 111,116, 120-121, 125, 130 (top), 131 (bottom), 136-137, 139, 146-147, 147 (center), 148-149, 151 (bottom), 154 a 159, 170-171, 181, 182 (top right and bottom), 186 a 188, 190 a 193, 196-197, 208, 211 a 218, 225 (top), 227 (top), 229 (bottom), 231 (top), 232-233, 240-241, 241(right), 242 a 245, 246-247 (top), 247 (bottom), 250-251, 254 (top right and bottom right), 255 (top left,right and bottom left).

ignacio urquiza - pgs. 11 (left), 56, 61 (bottom), 202, 221 (bottom),235 (right), 249.

jaime navarro - pg. 175.

joaquín cabeza - pgs. 32-33, 40-41, 106-107, 127.

jordi farré - pgs. 39, 99 a 101, 189, 209, 224-225.

jorge rodríguez almanza - pgs. 3. 83, 123, 223, 228-229 (top), 230 (bottom).

jorge taboada - pg. 222.

josé ignacio gonzález manterola - pgs. 60 (top left), 65, 248-249, 254 (top left).

lars herrmann - pgs. 28 (top left), 29.

lourdes legorreta - pgs. 134-135.

luis gordoa - pgs. 4-5, 6 (right), 66-67, 105, 114-115, 126-127, 130 (bottom), 131 (top), 179 (top), 182 (top left), 200-201, 201 (right), 220.

mayan jinich - pgs. 55 (top), 57, 94 (top left), 128-129, 142, 234 (left).

mauricio avramow - pgs. 52-53, 234-235.

michael calderwood - pgs. 45 (right), 194 (bottom), 195 (bottom), 198-199, 200 (left).

mito covarrubias - pgs. 6 (left), 9, 14-15, 58-59, 92, 203.

moda in casa - pgs. 54 (top), 54-55 (bottom).

pablo fernández del valle - pgs. 48-49, 84.

paul czitrom - pgs. 44-45, 62-63, 70-71, 80, 86-87, 90-91, 96-97, 113, 124, 160, 162-163, 166, 236, 238-239, 246 (bottom).

pedro luján - pgs. 168-169.

pedro riveroll - pg. 187.

rolando white - pgs. 75 (right), 78-79, 152-153.

sandra pérez nieto - pgs. 132-133.

santiago barreiro - pgs. 26, 28 (top right), 68, 122.

sebastián saldívar - pgs. 16, 37, 74 (left), 74-75, 76, 117, 141, 172-173, 174, 178-179, 237 (bottom), 240 (left), 254 (bottom left)

studio azurro - pgs. 24-25.

vicente san martín bautista - pg. 94 (top right and bottom).

Se terminó de imprimir en el mes de Enero del 2007 en China. El cuidado de la edición estuvo a cargo de AM Editores S.A. de C.V.